It Works for Me, Flipping the Classroom

Shared Tips for Effective Teaching

By Hal Blythe, Charlie Sweet, & Russell Carpenter

NEW FORUMS

NEW FORUMS PRESS INC.

Published in the United States of America

by New Forums Press, Inc.1018 S. Lewis St.

Stillwater, OK 74074

www.newforums.com

Copyright © 2015 by New Forums Press, Inc.

Library of Congress Cataloging-in-Publication Data Pending

This book may be ordered in bulk quantities at discount from New Forums Press, Inc., P.O. Box 876, Stillwater, OK 74076 [Federal I.D. No. 73 1123239]. Printed in the United States of America.

ISBN 10: 1-58107-280-5

ISBN 13: 978-1-581072-80-8

Table of Contents

Acknowledgments

For the eighth time, we need to thank scholars from around the country who took the time to write contributions for this book. We also need to recognize our publisher, Doug Dollar, who responds to our queries with timeliness and thoughtfulness. Gregg Wentzell of Miami University of Ohio proved invaluable in helping us solicit submissions. As usual, Susan Weaver of the University of the Cumberlands and DeDe Wohlfarth of Spalding University encouraged a number of faculty members to contribute. Finally, we are very appreciative of having a quality Graduate Assistant like Kelsey Strong, who provides the scholarly backbone of this edition.

Preface

Like Poe's narrator who begins "Ligeia" with the comment that "I cannot, for my soul, remember how, when, or even precisely where, I first became acquainted with the lady Ligeia," we cannot recall the precise situation, moment, or locale of our first confrontation with the concept of flipping the classroom. Unlike Poe's narrator, we cannot blame long years passing, a feeble memory (well, maybe), or even an addiction to opium for our ignorance.

We think our lives intersected with classroom flipping at the beginning of our careers. You see, we all come from a background in English studies where the nature of the beast, whether in writing or lit classes, is to assign primary and secondary sources as homework and then during class to discuss the material as well as provide opportunities for active learning responses (e.g., groups, reflections, additional media).

In short, in some form or other, we have always flipped our classroom, so all the recent academic hype on that methodology seems just that—hype. Back then, did we flip the classroom exactly the way the current research describes the methodology? Of course not.

The biggest change, though, in our discipline's traditional way of teaching and what flipping means today is technology. The development of the Internet as well as computers and software programs has basically outpaced even the most ardent flippers' attempts to participate in what we called in one of our previous New Forums books, *Teaching Applied Creative Thinking* (2013), "a techtonic shift."

Which brings up a good question—in 2015, what do we mean by the concept of flipping the classroom? In our view a flipped classroom has two components:

Out-of-Class: what do faculty and students do between class meetings—i.e., what are their respective assignments?

In Class: what do faculty and students do while the class is meeting—i.e., what activities are involved and what are the roles of the two groups?

Traditionally, pre-/post-class is devoted to "homework," and class time focuses on activities (though, truthfully, this period was once devoted to pure lecture). Flippers are fond of saying that in the new model, these two major duties are reversed or "flipped."

As usual, with the "It Works For Me" series, we have asked colleagues from across the country to contribute their knowledge, whether it's an overview or a particular tip. Not per usual, this book has a third author/editor as Charlie and Hal, who produced the first seven books in the series, are joined by their recent co-author. Rusty Carpenter arrived at Eastern Kentucky University in 2009, and since that time he has co-authored the *Introduction to Applied Creative Thinking* (2012), *Teaching Applied Creative Thinking* (2013), the Creativity Cafe column for *National Teaching & Learning Forum,* as well as half-a-dozen published articles.

As usual we have allowed writers to use the accepted reference formats of their of their disciplines.

In short, collaboration seems to work as well as flipping the classroom.

Introduction

I do not as I ought
I teach how I was taught.

Perhaps the above couplet should serve as a confession for new higher education faculty. Having not been prepared in graduate school by their disciplines in pedagogical effectiveness, especially in some of the recent contributions by neuro-scientists, they fall back on the format of their last teaching experience, the graduate school seminar. How often, they should ask, is this approach going to be effective in lower-division classrooms with less motivated and less prepared students?

As the titles for our last four books for New Forums—*It Works For Me, Creatively* (2011); *Introduction to Applied Creative Thinking* (2012); *Teaching Applied Creative Thinking* (2013); and *Achieving Excellence in Teaching* (2014)—make clear, we have focused on pedagogy, creative thinking, or both, and one simple synthesis of their content suggests that a key element of creativity, **taking risks**, is essential to becoming an excellent teacher. Yet taking risks, experimenting with various delivery methods, is fraught with peril for a number of reasons:

Most people are risk averse. When they come to the proverbial fork in the road, they would prefer not to take the one less travelled.

Most new faculty members spend the first five or six years of their post-grad school existence running the gauntlet known as tenure and promotion. Neither their student nor peer evaluations tend to reward classroom innovation.

Classroom experimentation demands hard work. Falling back on old notes, even those of your graduate professors, is easier.

Most new faculty members aren't very aware of the most recent pedagogical research.

Confronting a recent approach such as flipping the classroom becomes even more difficult as the methodology is so new that not enough time has passed for longitudinal studies. In fact, some circles view the flipping approach as a fad, so who wants to waste their tenure time on the pedagogical equivalent of pet rocks and mullet hairdos? And, unfortunately, by the time one is granted tenure and promotion, adhering to that steady course developed under the department's watchful eye is the safest road toward another promotion and a career at Higher Education University.

On the other hand, flipping the classroom offers several incentives.

On the risk-reward ratio, the <u>odds favor risk</u>. In fact, one way for newer faculty to justify the flipping experiment might be to play the "Stays current" card. Almost every P&T document has a section about staying current, and while many only apply that concept to discipline-specific knowledge, it makes just as much sense to apply it to pedagogy. In fact, the *NMC Horizon Report: 2014 Higher Education Edition* lists the Flipped Classroom as one of its three "Important Developments in Education Technology for Higher Education" and provides it with a Time-to-Adoption Horizon of "One Year or Less."

The flipped classroom approach almost <u>guarantees an active learning approach,</u> which, as we point out in *Achieving Excellence in Teaching,* has been research-proven to be more effective in promoting deep learning than its famous predecessor, the Lecture Method. With the flipping approach, classroom time is devoted to active exercises rather than passive note-taking.

The flipped classroom approach <u>confronts students at their technological level</u>. In order to provide students with homework, faculty are forced to develop a higher level of technological expertise, overcoming what the aforementioned *NMC Horizon Report* refers to as the problem of "low digital fluency of faculty." At the same time, such methods as creating videos, developing PowerPoints, and using new software programs don't demand faculty members possess a post-baccalaureate degree in technology.

The flipped classroom can provide <u>greater student access to the course</u>. K-12s have already discovered the ability to defeat snow days and illnesses through the technological delivery of classroom assignments. Higher education faculty can use it the same way as well as providing at least a partial answer to the student who has cut class and asks, "Did I miss anything?" Furthermore, with Title IX now requiring higher education to treat pregnancy as a disability, the flipped classroom provides expectant mothers with aid as well as a partial alternative to classroom attendance.

The flipped classroom allows senior faculty <u>one solution to burnout</u>. Re-invent yourself by flipping your classroom. Flippers cannot use yellowed notes to teach their classes.

For us, always possessing a nothing ventured-nothing gained attitude, flipping seemed natural, but if you have doubts, here's a suggestion. Choose a course where you teach two sections (preferably during the same semester), flip one and keep the other as you have been teaching. At the end of the semester, ask yourself and your students, which approach produced deep learning. Do an assessment, and write the research up as a piece of the scholarship of teaching and learning (SOTL). Congratulations! You just became a scholar-teacher.

I. Preparation for the Flipped Class Experience

How might faculty prepare to teach a flipped course? Better yet, what goes into the preparation process? The tips featured in this section focus on the work that takes place before the instructor enters the classroom. Offering perspective on such challenges as harnessing student creativity in the flipped classroom, designing projects for flipping the hybrid course, and experiences gleaned from participating in a flipping learning community, the tips will lead you through ideas that you can implement (or test) for your flipped classroom.

This section will serve as a useful foundation before you dive into the flipped course. The tips in this section are ideal for those new to flipping and veteran flippers alike. Taken together, this set of cases offers just the right amount of information to begin your planning process. Individually, though, the tips will provide you with the inside look on the planning it takes to implement a flipped classroom.

To Flip or Not to Flip; Is That My Only Choice?

Reports that students earn higher grades and increase critical thinking in flipped classrooms can make even the most reluctant instructor consider flipping. Should you flip? To address this question, we need to take a step back and look at what is meant by a flipped classroom. As currently described, a flipped classroom is one in which foundational information is moved outside of the classroom through readings, recorded mini-lectures, or videos. Class time is then used to help students apply the information through in-class activities, working through problems, or engaging in higher levels of critical thinking. In this model, you might expect students engaged in activities instead of lectures during class.

This type of flipped classroom might work well for those courses where information can be readily digested by students independently. That is, introductory psychology students can be expected to read their textbook outside of class and learn most terminology provided. For these students, then, a flipped approach might work very well, allowing class time to be devoted to helping students apply the information in a novel setting. For example, introductory students might read about Kohlberg's levels of moral development outside of class, and class time might then be devoted to students reading vignettes and determining what level of moral development is depicted.

Alternatively, a class that is highly technical, one in which students may have great difficulty digesting the material independently, may not be seen as appropriate for a flipped approach. In introductory psychology, for example, students have a great deal of difficulty understanding basic learning theory even after repeatedly reading it. For this topic, the lecture may play a critical role in helping students understand these concepts.

As you may have noted, both examples came from the same introductory psychology course. That is, there are times even within a course where 'flipping' may be appropriate and other times where 'flipping' is not as appropriate. Although this situation may seem contradictory, it truly is not. The goal is to ensure student learning. The flipped classroom model asks students to spend time outside of class preparing for the class session itself. This outside-of-class preparation may, at times, need to be supplemented by in-class short lectures that specifically address topics that students need clarified. Rather than lecturing for 60 minutes, professors may need to lecture for 10-15 minutes on very precise topics that assessment suggests students are failing to understand independently. Of course, such mini-lectures may be combined with in-class activities more commonly used to engage students in higher-level critical thinking. In truth, then, the question is not whether we flip or do not flip, but rather to what degree do we flip to meet the learning needs of our students?

Robin K. Morgan, Indiana University Southeast
Nathanael G. Mitchell, Spalding University
Norah Chapman, Spalding University
Acknowledgement: Thanks to Dave Morgan, Ph.D. for his contributions to editing.

Start with an Instructional Design Theoretical Construct

"Flipping" is a non-traditional way for teachers to sequence instruction. The activities that once took place in the classroom during the direct instruction phase of teaching are now made available to the students outside of the traditional class period so they can access that content and information outside of school. The classroom time with the teacher where the direct instruction was once provided is now freed up for activities and assignments that enhance the content, thus allowing for a greater depth and breadth of student curricular engagement.

Although the sequence and vehicle of transmission of the curricular content for the student have changed, the need for the instructor to provide a structured theoretical construct to guide the development of a sound instructional unit has not. Teachers still need to have a solid instructional design underpinning for their units of instruction to be most effective. In fact, a "flipped" instructional situation makes it even more incumbent upon the instructor to have a solid theoretical understanding and foundation to the way concepts are taught, discussed, developed, assessed, and evaluated.

Faculty attempting to "flip" their instruction should spend a great deal of time in reflection and introspection about what they are currently doing in the classroom; why they are doing those things; and the reasons for the way they structure expectations, experiences, information, and assessment. Methods, materials, sequencing, pacing, presentation, and groupings all need to be considered and explored.

Once these items have been considered, faculty members should compare their current instructional practices to their theoretical constructs of learning, with a keen eye to the way these constructs align to a theory of instructional design. Once instructors are confident in their insights, they should diagram them out and compare them to the research related to the instructional design model they are predisposed to using. These diagrams are a helpful tool to ensure that small but important aspects to the instructional and assessment sequences currently utilized are not lost when the "flipping" occurs.

Working together with a peer who understands your style of teaching, who has the content knowledge to help identify subtle areas of change, who recognizes what you are trying to accomplish with a "flipped" format, and who will give you an honest appraisal of your efforts is an incredible support that should be utilized. Have this person come in and observe your instruction prior to "flipping." Then have that colleague go through the same analysis of your instruction described in the previous paragraph. Compare that insight to your own, and once you have a clear and accurate understanding of your current structure and presentation, you can then start designing your new "flipped" sequence of instruction.

Take the diagrams of your current instructional format and place them in your current instructional sequential order. Once that task is completed, compare your sequence with that of your peer's sequential order. Edit your current instructional sequence and format as necessary to incorporate your colleague's ideas into your own. Once that task is done, you should be ready to "flip" your instruction.

Using your instructional design theory as a template, rearrange your instructional format so the content delivery and direct instruction is temporally placed at a time when the "flipping" is to occur. Take the remaining diagram contents and fill in the rest of your instructional sequence and activities that will occur during the school day. Pay close attention to make sure that subtle pieces of your current instructional sequence are not lost in your new "flipped" format.

Have your trusted peer look over the new "flipped" template for instruction to ensure that you have accomplished the transformations that you desire. When all of the pieces from your traditional instructional format have been slotted into the new "flipped" instructional format, and your feedback from your peer coach is positive, you should be ready to develop lessons based upon these new teaching and learning activities.

Start slowly. Be reflective in the selection and utilization of your methods, materials, presentation, sequencing, and time allotment during your initial "flipped" forays. Obtain formative feedback from your students about their insights to the new format, and take their counsel seriously. When appropriate, incorporate their ideas into your instructional format. During all of these activities, go back to your theory of instructional design. Are you incorporating the required elements during the "flipped" process? If not, identify the steps necessary so the important aspects of the instructional sequence are not lost.

Continue to work towards more and more "flipped" instructional opportunities, but realize that this format may not be appropriate for all content. If you do not have the time to develop appropriate content or online resources do not exist for the content, you might have to revert to the traditional instructional sequence. When revisiting the traditional format, make sure that you alert learners to the change in format. This warning helps them understand the expectations that you have for their learning so they can rearrange their expectations for their understandings.

Continue to work collaboratively with trusted peers to hone your focus, content, pacing, methods, materials, and expectations for "flipped" instruction. Over time, with collegial support, you should be able to develop quite a library of resources that can be shared across instructors, thus enhancing the "flipped" experience for everyone within the program.

"Flipped" instruction has the potential to support student learning in a way few other interventions have been able to in the past. Educators attempting to "flip" their instruction need to pay attention to the pedagogical and andragogical aspects of the process and not get lost or enamored with the technological capabilities of the new learning format. Attending to the instructional design theory that they currently utilize in their programs and recognizing those elements in the new "flipped" system when direct instruction is provided is important to ensure that the "flipped" instruction maintains its rigor and relevance for the learner.

Mark E. Deschaine, Central Michigan University

Flipping Your Syllabus

Congratulations! You have made the decision to flip your classroom and, most likely, spent significant time carefully designing out-of-class materials and in-class activities that align with one another to create a rich learning environment for your students. Do you really think that old syllabus is going to cut it?

The syllabus is the first impression students have of your class. Traditionally, students expect to come to the first day of class and have the professor review the syllabus. However, this approach runs counter to everything we are trying to do with a flipped classroom. If we are serious about flipping, we must also flip our syllabus – and what we do on the first day of class.

On the syllabus, we include a brief statement describing what students can expect from our class. Will there be lectures? Will students be expected to participate? Will students be expected to work in groups? Our syllabi are carefully constructed to provide students a sense of what we are like as professors and what our expectations are of our students.

Prior to the first day of class, an email can be sent to the class, asking students to read the syllabus and to come to class prepared to discuss it. Adding an online 'syllabus quiz' is a great way to ensure that students have read the syllabus prior to coming to class and to set the expectation that, in this class, students will be responsible for completing work outside the classroom. Alternatively, students might be given a scavenger list of questions that can be completed by reading the syllabus such as, "Who should you call if you can't open an online quiz?" Furthermore, assessment of gaining basic knowledge from reading materials outside of class is vital to a successfully flipped class. Therefore, starting that process with assessing student knowledge of the syllabus may be a good way for students to become oriented for the remainder of the semester.

Flipping allows for more applied learning and discussion throughout the semester, and flipping the syllabus allows for more applied learning of the syllabus on the first day as well. During class, students can be placed into groups to work on more "applied" or difficult questions/vignettes that relate to student issues and what should be done about them per syllabus policies. Students might be given a vignette, for example, of a student who has a documented learning need, or has arrived late to more than one class. As a group, the students might review policies on the syllabus for dealing with this issue and discuss the purposes behind certain policies. Additionally, students could be asked to explore more in depth the objectives of the course and how they might apply to their lives, currently or in their future careers.

In short, flipping the syllabus provides an important model to students for how the class will be structured the rest of the semester and ensures students understand the content in the syllabus. A side benefit is that students begin to interact with one another, setting the stage for more successful small group activities.

Nathanael G. Mitchell, Spalding University
Robin Morgan, Indiana University Southeast
Norah Chapman, Spalding University
Acknowledgement: Thanks to Dave Morgan, Ph.D. for his contributions to editing.

Gradual Approach to Flipping

Although the flipped classroom model has been around for years, this time may be the first you, personally, have decided to flip a course. Rather than become overwhelmed with the idea that flipping your course has to happen all at once, consider that there may be a methodical way to gradually go about it. Before you jump in with both feet, consider these suggestions:

- **Review your course student learning outcomes**: Good course design begins with measurable course student learning outcomes. It will be difficult to create an effective flipped class if you do not have good student learning outcomes in place. Your campus teaching and learning center (CTL) is a great resource for helping you to develop or polish these outcomes.

- **Choose 3-5 topics/days to flip**: Flipping the entire class on your first attempt is overwhelming! For each day you flip, you will need to create high quality materials for students to review outside of class, and you will need to create in-class activities that align with those materials. If the materials are not high quality or not well aligned, your flip may not be effective. It's much easier to flip 3-5 class sessions initially and then build across semesters until you are prepared to totally flip.
- **Hold Students Accountable**: If students are expected to review materials outside of class, you must create some method to assess whether they have completed this work. The easiest method is probably an online quiz that students would complete prior to class. Starting each class with a short quiz also works well. Many instructors require students to participate in a forum discussion prior to class addressing the material. Of course, for this strategy to be effective, the instructor needs to create a good forum discussion question and then grade responses utilizing a rubric. Other brief assignments may also work well, such as asking students to complete a video recording describing what they have learned in their own words or what they would do if they had to teach a concept to someone outside of the field.
- **Develop Materials**: You will have two sets of materials to develop: outside of class materials and inside of class materials. It may seem that all you will need to do is to record your lectures and post them. This approach has not been found to be highly effective. Instead, you may wish to look online for short videos, create short, narrated PowerPoints, and identify specific readings that address major topics. This action will take some time and effort. The materials will need to be developed in conjunction with your assessment process for ensuring that students are held accountable for reviewing these materials prior to class. Inside of class materials will also need to be developed. Such materials may consist of activities, discussions, debates, or other tasks that allow students to be engaged and to focus on higher-level critical thinking. The materials need to be carefully aligned with outside of class materials so that students can see the connection between what they are asked to do before class and what they are asked to do in class.
- **Integrate Assessment**: Whatever your method of class assessment – exams, quizzes, papers – the assessment process needs to value the skills students are to develop in their in-class activities as much as the materials they review prior to coming to class. Developing assessments that achieve this result requires significant effort. These assessments should also clearly relate to the course student learning objectives.

Robin Morgan, Indiana University Southeast
Nathanael G. Mitchell, Spalding University

Norah Chapman, Spalding University
Acknowledgement: Thanks to Dave Morgan, Ph.D. for his contributions to editing.

Creating a Personal Welcome for Your Flipped Class

Although students in flipped classes meet face-to-face with instructors, the students' first exposure to the class very likely will be in the course management system. First impressions matter! You may consider several methods for making a good first impression, including embedding engaging pictures that represent the course content or using a written or recorded greeting that may be helpful for students to get to know the course and you as their instructor. One particularly effective way for capturing all such intentions is to develop a welcome video. Creating an engaging video that welcomes students to the course allows faculty to personalize their course and develop a more welcoming environment. Additionally, by providing the welcome video you set the expectation that students are expected to engage in the course management system and the course content outside of class (an essential component to a flipped class).

Below, we provide some basic tips for creating a welcome video that will ensure that this first impression is a positive one.

- **Nonverbals rule!** Making eye contact and an open body posture are inviting. On a recording, look directly at the camera so as to appear on screen as if you are looking at the viewer. Although it is tempting to read notes or to cross your arms, neither conveys the warmth and connection you want.
- **Be careful with humor**: What seems funny to you may be offensive to some of your students or simply come across as pathetic. Be relevant and authentic in a way that is professional, while being aware of the potential reactions students may have to the content of your humor.
- **Lighting and Background**: You don't need to use a professional studio, but do make sure shadows don't obscure your face or gestures. Avoiding distracting backgrounds is probably also wise. This prohibition does not mean you need to record videos in your office. Backgrounds that are relevant and incorporated into the video work wonderfully. For example, one of Nora's favorite welcome videos was of a geology professor whose recording was actually done in the Grand Canyon.
- **Dress**: When on screen, be mindful that what you are wearing may have an effect on the appearance of the video. For example, your outfit may blend in with the background of your video or may be so patterned or bright that it can create a glare or be distracting. Darker colors that do not blend in with the background may be a safe way to go.

- **Professional but not formal**: People who don't like being videotaped can easily become wooden and stiff when creating a video. The goal is to convey your personal warmth, but as a professional. It may be helpful to practice your video several times before doing your final "take." Going through your video script or outline with others whom you trust to get feedback may be a good first step.
- **Convey Passion:** Make sure that your passion for teaching and the subject/content are conveyed appropriately in the video. Students would rather learn from someone who cares about the content and enjoys what they do for a living. Why do you love to teach this class? How is it relevant to your field and interests? Why is it relevant to your students' lives now and in the future?
- **Short and sweet**! Figure out what you want to say – scripts are good – and keep your video to less than 10 minutes. Numerous studies have shown that students respond best to shorter videos.

Many tools can be used to create your welcome video. We will briefly review two that are fairly easy for a novice faculty member: Present Me and Echo 360 Personal Capture. Both of these tools allow faculty to develop a video from their desktop. An attractive feature of both tools is that each allows the faculty member to utilize a split screen with the camera image on one screen and a PowerPoint on screen capture on another screen.
- Present Me (https://present.me/content/) allows the creation of a video with simply a camera and a microphone. Several types of files may be uploaded – PowerPoint, PDF, Google Doc, Prezi – to be used within the video. The process is simple: click RECORD and begin. The editing process is limited, but allows you to start, stop, and delete without much effort. Sharing the finished product can be accomplished by embedding the video into your course management site, by emailing a link, or by creating a private subdomain.
- Echo 360 Active Learning Platform provides both lecture capture and a personal capture option. The Personal Capture option provides a fast and easy method of creating a Welcome Video. It shares many features with Present Me – it can upload many types of documents, minor editing is possible, and many ways exist to share the finished video. With Echo 360 Personal Capture, it is also possible to use analytics to see which students have watched the welcome video.

Creating a personal welcome using such technological tools can provide an opportunity to start your course in a meaningful way. Students begin to build an impression of the course and you as their instructor. Therefore, create a first impression that will hook them and help them engage with you and the class right away.

Norah Chapman, Spalding University
Robin Morgan, Indiana University Southeast
Nathanael G. Mitchell, Spalding University
Acknowledgement: Thanks to Dave Morgan, Ph.D. for his contributions to editing.

Ultra TLC to Flip without Fizzles and Flops

Flipping the classroom can offer many ways for students to succeed in a creative environment. Unfortunately, it can also provide many ways for students who are challenged by disabilities, poor academic preparation, competing schedule demands, or lack of resources to fizzle and fail without notice until a project is due. The following ideas, which have worked for me to provide a structure for personalized support in flipped classrooms with 15 to 50 students, are based on universal design practices of presenting material in multiple ways, allowing multiple forms of student expression, and motivating students to learn (CAST, 2013).

A simple first-day survey about learning style preferences, confidence, group skills, computer skills, and access can raise red flags about student success with particular approaches. Another resource is the Epistemic Belief Inventory, which assesses self-efficacy, motivation, and self-regulation (Conn, English, Scheffler, & Hall, 2011). These tools offer insights that enable the professor to better understand individual student needs. Outreach should extend to everyone, but some students might need extra attention. Providing time for students to identify a study partner can help to create community. One way to create diverse groups is to have people sign up by interest in a preset list of topics. A safeguard for group work is a carefully written group project rubric that includes successful collaboration and input from all in the group as assessed factors. This rubric places greater social responsibility on group participants and increases the likelihood that the super student will encourage the at-risk student. With this approach as the basis, I totally FLIP, i.e., offer frequent feedback in a learner-centered pedagogy that is individualized through well planned structure.

Frequent feedback is critical in shaping student learning as well as a sense of efficacy and connection. Vardi (2013) found that feedback is most effective when it points to the next step and when it can be used immediately for revision. Encouragement and praise can help to raise students' expectations, but sometimes finding something to praise requires a magnifying glass. However, even a one sentence essay can result in "Your main point is very clear. I would like to hear more about your reasoning. Why do you think that _____ ?" or "This is good work. I saw only a couple of minor grammar issues, such as subject / verb agreement. I would be happy to look at it with you or the tutoring center offers free consultations." I require at least very rough drafts on all papers for five points on formal assignments, but give feedback and revision opportunity even on informal assignments. "I will be happy to regrade if you want to make changes" seems to foster a constructive attitude in the student. Oddly, very few students actually resubmit, but the quality of future work seems to improve quickly.

Learner-centered material addresses a variety of learning styles. Many students do not have strong reading skills, so offloading entire chapters seems unfair. Moreover, the current trend in teaching and learning is to focus on targeted short readings that are reinforced with assignments. Adding short videos, individual or group projects, and reflection address as multiple learning preferences. Students seem to especially prefer options that involve applying the course concepts or material to interviews or research with family, friends, or even professionals.

Invite students to contact you and, if feasible, establish appointments to have individual contact with each student. The flipped classroom sometimes can increase feelings of marginalization for students who are not prepared for academic success. This insecurity is potentially compounded for students in a college setting if the college community does not reflect the size, values, speech, or activities of home. If students do not contact me, I contact them if they miss class or an assignment, especially at the beginning of the term. This process is an established practice in retention, especially for at-risk students.

Plan ahead so that material and skills required for the coursework prepare them for future professional activities. Students even appreciate quizzes and tests when they understand that they help to prepare them for multiple choice exams at the end of course, end of program, graduate entrance, or professional certification/licensure requirements. On the other hand, many students simply do not do well on multiple choice tests. Talley (2013) found that practice tests increase retention and performance. In addition to mastery of the material, they help students to develop confidence while increasing overall test-taking skills. Some might argue that this "dumbs down" the material. Actually, it does the opposite. It gears up the learner.

Many of these ideas might sound utopian, but flipping the classroom is not business as usual. It provides time to give the extra attention to those who tend to disappear otherwise. The best students used to be the only ones to come to the office, but they all seem comfortable now. Paybacks are not always immediate. One of our recent graduates said that he did not feel that he belonged in college and did not care, but the memories of my seemingly unsuccessful efforts to reach him 7 years ago kept drawing him back. He is now applying to graduate school. We do not know what shadows of past experiences our students bring, but shining a light brings clarity to individual importance and capability.

References

CAST (2013) Universal Design and the Flipped Classroom. National Center on Universal Design for Learning. Retrieved from http://www.cast.org/udl/

Conn, S., English, J., Scheffler, F. & Hall, S. (2011, August). Student epistemic belief data in course design: A research-based approach to improve student academic success. Information Systems Education Journal, 9(3), 9-20. Retrieved from http://isedj.org/2011-9/N3/ISEDJVol9No3.pdf

Talley, C. & Scherer, S. (2013). The enhanced flipped classroom: Increasing academic performance with student-recorded lectures and practice testing in a "flipped" STEM course. Journal of Negro Education, 82(3), 339-347. Retrieved from doi: 10.7709/jnegroeducation.82.3.0339

Vardi, I. (2013, August). Effectively feeding forward from one written assignment task to the next. Assessment and Evaluation in Higher Education, 38(5), 599-610. Retrieved from doi: 10.1080/02602938.2012.670197

Susan Weaver, University of the Cumberlands

Effective Integration of Course Syllabus and Online Video Technology to Explain Student Role in Flipped Classroom Design for Blended Course

In March of 2012, I created a blended course comprised of both face-to-face classroom learning and online learning titled *Management 443 Organizational Project*. This course utilizes a flipped classroom design for degree completion students. This course requires that students meet six times during a semester and create a written four chapter project to systemically improve an organization. I will discuss a strategy that I have successfully used to help students understand what a flipped classroom is and what their role in the flipped classroom design will be.

In the MGT 443 syllabus, I have created a separate subsection of content that provides a written three-step process explaining to students their required role. This content is provided below:

MGT 443 `Flipped' Course Design for Weekly Activities: Face-to-Face & Blended

In this course, students meet six times over the course of the entire third semester of their program. Each face-to-face meeting will be held on a particular day of the week for weeks 49, 55, 61, 67, 71 and 72 (please see your cohort weekly schedule for calendar times to meet for these weeks of the Organizational Leadership program).

To complete the weekly activities for this course for the first four of six meetings (Weeks 49, 55, 61 and 67), complete, in sequence, the following three steps:

Step 1: *Go to Moodle course site. Review and complete all online assignments for assigned week of class **prior** to meeting face-to-face. Prior to face-to face class meeting, also complete all required chapter readings assigned for that particular week of class.*

Step 2: *Bring to face-to-face class meetings three hard copies of assigned chapters 1, 2, 3, or 4 drafts.*

Step 3: *After receiving feedback from fellow students and your instructor during face-to-face class meeting, use that feedback to continue to improve each chapter draft and within one week of class time, submit your revised and improved chapter draft to the Moodle site for instructor review and feedback.*

I have also created a three-minute video in the online Moodle area for this blended course wherein I explain these same three steps and also provide additional information of what a flipped classroom is. This video was developed with the assistance of the Center for Online Learning (COL) at Fresno Pacific University. The COL arranged for the professional staging and filming of this video, along with the inclusion of graphics to illustrate the three steps. The information provided in both the written syllabus and the online portion explaining the three-step process for this "flipped" course is essentially the same.

This flipped classroom format provides degree-completion students the opportunity to use online course learning and assigned readings to create drafts of their written chapters outside of the classroom environment. These chapter drafts are then brought by the student to the face-to-face class, where they receive feedback on ways to improve them. After receiving feedback provided by classmates and their instructor, students are given an additional week to improve their chapter draft a second time.

In conclusion, the strategy of integrating different modalities of learning in both the syllabus and use of video technology in the Moodle area of this blended course helps reinforce and more clearly explain to students what a flipped classroom design is and what their required role will be.

Breck A. Harris, Fresno Pacific University

Steps for Flipping Your Classroom Using Project Based Learning

A **Flipped Classroom** engages students to learn through natural interests. When paired with the PBL strategy (Project Based Learning), student engagement further drives learning through choice. No matter the content or the age of student, blending a Flipped Classroom with the PBL Strategy uses the following steps:

Teacher Step 1: Pre-Planning Decisions: Choose a unit or topic; then brainstorm!

Think about all the units or topics that are required for the course. What ideas come to mind? Are some topics easier to link to projects?

Example: K-12 linking science, literacy, creativity

The project started with teaching in an inner-city middle school facing reorganization. How can the desire to learn link with content? The students were frightened of or angry with school. Those who could read were often 2-3 years below grade level. Previously, my teaching included high school Earth Science, Biology, and Art when the district suddenly moved me to the troubled middle school. Now, I found myself in a Related Arts Wheel with 9 week rotations and my subject, art, linked to the literacy strand. This strategy uses it all! Here are some sites to get you started!

Students: http://sciencespot.net/Pages/kdzbiopond.html
Teachers: http://bie.org/about/what_pbl
http://www.nextgenscience.org/
http://nationalartsstandards.org/
http://www.corestandards.org/ELA-Literacy/RST/6-8/
http://www.nextgenscience.org/sites/ngss/files/Appendix%20M%20Connections
http://www.nga.gov/content/ngaweb.html
http://store.doverpublications.com/0486410358.html?
Bernhard, A. *Freshwater Pond Coloring Book,* Dover Books

Teacher Step 2: Designing Learning

As a school, we adopted the strategy of reading across the curriculum, linking contents in any way we could. My thought was *how can I tie in literacy, science, and visual art with enough motivation to inspire learning?* The answer came with a page from a coloring book on pond life!

From that page, I then identified the standards that were required for the grades. These had to be displayed for anyone to read throughout the unit or topic.

> 1-**Pre-teaching**: Students read a simple paragraph, underline or highlight key terms.
> Discuss the meaning of those terms, asking students to state in their own words. Watch videos--using the Internet, classroom, or lab computers--that include identified terms.
> 2-**Group Students** into small groups of 3-5.
> Think about natural interests and abilities of the students. Make different divisions for different units or topics of study. Remember, the students should want to work with their group.

The grouping is a good way to develop or strengthen leadership as well as writing and research skills. In the art class, I made sure each group had someone who had stronger drawing skills.

Teacher Step 3: Educating Students

> 3-**Explain the PBL Process** to the students, stating that they get to choose how they learn and what product they create. Support the basic learning previously used to introduce the topic by allowing students to pick and choose from a bookmarked or saved list of articles, videos, images, etc.
> 4-Student Learning occurs through group work where they identify questions, write a list of their questions, and then brainstorm how or where to find answers. Supply 2 lists: **Suggested Activities/Websites** that are student friendly for the groups to use and **Possible Products** to present to the class on a set date.

Students direct their learning using cooperative strategies. Each group should create 3 things: a list of learning questions, a learning plan that fits within the class timeline, and a product to present to the class.

Student Step 1

Identify roles each student has in the group: leader, recorder, checker, webmaster, artist, etc.

Remember each student must contribute to the final product and help present to the class. Brainstorm, identify questions, and list **Learning Questions**.

Student Step 2

Identify natural interests of your group: do you like games, art, experiments, presentations, or writing? For each question think about what you need to do, look up other resources, find pictures, watch a video for more information. How will your group show what was learned?

Discuss with the whole class and your teacher. Make your decisions and create a plan including a timeline, the product, and materials. **The Learning Plan** needs to fit within your teacher's time allowed for this unit or subject.

Student Step 3

Each group then works for 2-3 days to create the **Product.** Products may take any form offered as a choice from the teacher.

Student Step 4

Present Product to the class. Presentations are short yet show what you have learned in a way that was interesting to you!

As students use this learning strategy, they become more independent and creative. If many ideas exist, each group may bring their ideas to the whole class as they process their ideas toward final products. PBLs use student inquiry to develop a trail to find an answer. Instead of students filling in blanks, answering questions on a test, they work together to discover answers. With true inquiry comes innovation!

Karen McDonald Goldman, University of the Cumberlands

Go "Old School" with New Technology

Effective teaching is meeting students where they are and taking them where they need to go. There may have been a time that most students entering our courses could effectively read their textbooks. There may even have been a time that most of them could (and did!) successfully complete problems in the book to gain mastery of the material. For most of us, that time has passed, but we still (rightly) strive for the same learning objectives. Fortunately, new technologies can enable us to achieve these learning objectives with proven pedagogies.

The central tenet of this essay is that active learning, as embodied in "flipped classrooms," is a highly effective instructional method. The challenges we face are to provide our students effective means to prepare for class, effective classroom activities, and effective means to consolidate their in-class learning gains after class. Recognition of our students' actual preparation and use of modern technology have enabled development of a hybrid Just-in Time Teaching (JiTT) approach (Lage, Platt, & Treglia, 2000; Novak, Patterson, Gavrin, & Christian, 1999; Simkins and Maier, 2009) in organic chemistry that bears much similarity to the Thayer Method that has been used at West Point for almost two centuries (United States. General Accounting Office, 1975). Two years of this approach have seen significantly better student outcomes in organic chemistry compared to the prior five years of proficient lecturing. Exam averages have improved, with the most substantial improvement (4.5%) on the cumulative final. Most importantly, DFW rates have decreased from a consistent 26% to 9%.

This hybrid JiTT approach differs from traditional JiTT primarily in that greater support is given to students prior to class. Traditional JiTT typically guides students' pre-class reading of the textbook with 2-3 open-ended questions over the reading and a "muddiest point" question provides opportunity for the students to explain which material they struggle with the most. This hybrid JiTT approach has kept the "muddiest point" question, but replaces the 2-3 open-ended questions with:

- Detailed lists of learning objectives for each section of the textbook
- Tutorial online homework assignments
- One or two 5-10 minute electronic mini-lectures over the most challenging material.

The lists of learning objectives average about a half page per 90-minute class period. The online homework assignments are supplied by the textbook publisher (OWL, 2013). It was initially hoped that the mini-lectures wouldn't be necessary, but between weaknesses in student preparation and the textbook it quickly became clear that they are needed to prepare students for in-class activities. Mini-lectures are recorded using an electronic whiteboard application (Explain Everything, 2013). Students use a course management system (Moodle, 2013) to submit answers to the "muddiest" point questions.

Effective use of instructional time is at the core of the flipped classroom. This hybrid JiTT approach uses class time to answer students' "muddiest point" questions and reinforce their learning with group problem solving. Students self-arrange into groups of 3-4 for these activities. Two or three times per 90-minute class session three problems are presented with 2-3 groups working each problem. They are instructed to work individually for at least a minute, then work together to make sure that everyone in the group understands the solution. Group members take turns recording solutions using an electronic whiteboard application (Explain Everything, 2013) on iPads. These solutions are uploaded into a database in the course management system and at least one solution for each problem is reviewed and discussed with the class emphasizing process and reasoning. The use of electronic whiteboards in place of physical ones is useful for several reasons:

- Student fear of presenting their work publically is greatly diminished,
- Students are substantially more willing to think critically about their own work and that of others; and
- Students are able to review the solutions after class (below).

Review and consolidation of learning gains is still important after a flipped classroom session. This hybrid JiTT approach accomplishes review and consolidation primarily with homework questions from the textbook and online homework supplied by the publisher (OWL, 2013). Optional homework problems from the textbook are listed with the learning objectives (above) for each section of material. Required online homework is due at the beginning of each week (for the prior week's material). Students may also review their classmates' solutions to in-class group problems, though few choose to do so until the instructor comments upon their validity.

This hybrid JiTT approach works for me and my students. It's a little bit old and a little bit new, much like the flipped classroom itself. Students learn organic chemistry and become better readers (an increasingly ancient learning objective) using modern technology with which they are comfortable.

References

OWL (version 1.0) [Website]. Retrieved from http://cengage.com.

Lage, M. J., Platt, G. J., Treglia, M. (2000). Inverting the Classroom: A Gateway to Creating an Inclusive Learning Environment. *Journal of Economic Education*, 31(1), 30-43.

Moodle (version 2.5) [Website]. Retrieved from https://moodle.wittenberg.edu.

Explain Everything (version 2.31) [Mobile Application Software]. Retrieved from http://itunes.apple.com.

Novak, G. M., Patterson, E, T., Gavrin, A. D.; & Christian, W. (1999). Just-in-Time Teaching: Blending Active Learning with Web Technology. Upper Saddle River, NJ: Prentice-Hall.

Simkins, S., & Maier, M., Eds. (2009). Just in Time Teaching: Across the Disciplines, Across the Academy. Sterling, Va: Stylus Pub.

United States. General Accounting Office. (1975). Academic and military programs of the five service academies, Departments of Defense, Transportation, and Commerce: report to the Congress. Washington: U.S. General Accounting Office.

Justin B. Houseknecht, Wittenberg University

Harness Student Creativity and Expertise

In an ideal world a college professor's extensive experience in the classroom would translate directly into competence in developing effective online lectures. But the fact of the matter is that when it comes to creating online content, we are probably lagging substantially behind our students in our expectations of what constitutes a high-quality product and possibly in our familiarity with the technologies available for creating that content.

Our first attempt at delivering a flipped classroom experience was for a non-majors biology course. We developed a short run of video lectures and assigned them as homework, then used the reclaimed time for group work on a semester-long project. The trial generated mixed responses. Students enjoyed the increased in-class time for project work but were surprisingly negative in their responses to our lecture videos.

The videos we presented were simple voice-over slideshows, a format essentially chosen by default based on our limited knowledge of video creation. Students reported difficulty maintaining their attention and criticized the pacing as well as the video and audio quality.

Our breakthrough came when we realized that we were surrounded by potential guides to what students *would* find engaging and effective.

We reached out to undergraduate students in the Animation and Interactive Design majors at our university. After some short trial projects, we hired these students as content creation assistants to create a semester-long set of lectures for a non-majors environmental science course that we hoped to run entirely in a flipped classroom format.

The first step in the collaboration was creating a set of potential "modes" of content delivery that we could create given the technology that was available to us. These included filmed white-board lectures, animated slide shows, motion diagrams, professional animations, and newscaster-style presentations in which lecturers are filmed with content appearing alongside or behind their "talking head." This vastly expanded the range of possibilities available to us and allowed us to approach each module with a palette of options. It also helped us to understand the differences in production time for different modes of presentation and to fine-tune our plans accordingly.

Rather than doing a direct translation of our slide presentations, we set those aside and developed new lecture scripts from scratch, and then developed storyboards with the animation students to match those scripts. Storyboarding mostly consisted of the matching up of material to the different modes of delivery, with some light sketching of how figures and diagrams should appear on screen. We then gave the students our existing slides as resource material. Whereas we had previously recorded our lectures in Powerpoint, Camtasia, or using Adobe Captivate, students implemented Adobe Premier and After Effects to allow for more sophisticated custom animations and to facilitate the integration of videos, text, diagrams, and animation into the same video frame.

Over time several interesting things happened. First, students were able to teach the instructors quite a bit about video editing and production, a process that was much faster and more effective than the instructors attempting to learn that material on their own. One major benefit of this instructing is that it will allow future maintenance of course materials to be conducted by the instructor.

Second, students created a robust file system for holding source material, video clips, and project files based on their own professional training in the animation field. This under-appreciated aspect of digital design work is important in ensuring that course materials can be updated in the future without starting over from scratch.

Third, students very quickly grabbed onto some of the basics of presentation creation in an academic context and were able to begin participating in and contributing their own creativity to the content generation phase. They became both critics and co-creators of our lecture materials, influencing the modes of communication we chose, the kinds of diagrams and illustrations we used, and the overall timing and pacing of the content modules.

In order to assess our results, we began an intense surveying procedure as soon as we deployed the online modules in order to harvest student opinions. Using an online anonymous survey, we asked students to rate the particular modes of presentation that we used in terms of their:

- Ability to extract key information
- Ability to maintain focus/attention
- Ability to understand the context for the information presented
- Ability to retain that information
- Engagement with the material
- Enjoyment of the material.

Certainly, better ways to assess whether students are retaining information than to ask them exist, but the responses give us some guidance with which to move forward in terms of both content creation and assessment. Students are, after all, the most important stakeholder in this process. As this project progresses, we hope to begin measuring more directly the effect of different presentation styles on course learning outcomes. One additional item to note regarding student responses is that many students were highly impressed by the fact that much of the content they were viewing was generated by their peers. Our interpretation was that it generated a level of connection by providing a concrete example of how other (also non-major) students were able to connect deeply to the material.

It's hard to see how we could have completed the classroom flip without the student participation. Even if we had, the end product would have been much reduced in quality and effectiveness. We are currently working with the animation department to create a more formal, work-study supported role for upper-level animation students to be employed in a content-creation studio that can be accessed by any faculty members seeking to create electronic course materials.

Student energy and creativity are renewable resources that every educational institution possesses in abundance. We should use them to our advantage, especially when moving from the old and tried to the new and untried. Students are the ones who will be most affected by shifts in pedagogy. Let their insight help to shape how those pedagogies are deployed.

Jeffrey A. Klemens, Kanbar College of Design, Engineering, and Commerce
Christopher M. Pastore, Kanbar College of Design, Engineering, and Commerce
Michael S. Hudson, Kanbar College of Design, Engineering, and Commerce

Flipping the Hybrid Classroom Online: Projects and Conversations

Is it possible to flip your classroom and not know it? On the last day of my hybrid online graduate course on Achieving Excellence in College Teaching, we came together to share some food and synthesize what we have learned. One of my students surprised me with the observation that, "You have flipped your classroom." How so? "We met the first night to clarify assignments and to discuss the major projects, and then you asked us to read the entire book and complete the five assignments for the class. Each assignment built upon the previous one, and we only came together online to discuss our questions and concerns. You also provided mini-lectures through streaming video that clarified the research behind our textbook [*Achieving Excellence in College Teaching: A Practical Guide (2014)* by Sweet, C., Blythe, H., Phillips, B.]. That is what I call a flipped classroom."

This astute student articulated a new concept for many of his classmates, the flipped online classroom. Many online courses are video lectures and PowerPoint; others remind us of correspondence courses that are comprised of written materials and tests. The flipped classroom usually provides students with reading material and lectures as homework and allows for discussions that are interactive and active.

In my graduate class on Achieving Excellence in Teaching, the students' first assignment is to read the entire book so that we have something to discuss. My students also are involved with projects that require them to use the material in the book and to create a product. I give them feedback on each assignment, and then we have more things to discuss as a class. Each assignment builds upon previous learning. The mini-lectures reiterate the research from the book and clarify each individual project.

Another assignment is to create a self-improvement plan using the book's Rubric to Attain Teaching Excellence [RATE]. Students evaluate their skills using a Likert Scale to identify strengths, weaknesses, opportunities, and threats. The students use the analysis to create SMART specific, measurable, attainable, realistic and timely goals. The class then has specific things to discuss in a threaded online follow-up session on improving teacher effectiveness.

Flipping the hybrid online classroom allows the instructor to explain, demonstrate, guide, and enable [EDGE]. By reading the book, students have a good **explanation** of the research behind the theory and the mini lectures. Then they review what has been read. An explanation is also given for the project's purpose, while an excellent example of a successful project is provided as a **demonstration** of what is expected. Students are given **guided** practice by allowing them multiple attempts to complete the project. If the student's efforts are not high quality, then the assignment is returned electronically with feedback. Students are **enabled** to continue to improve their projects until the instructor is satisfied that they are the best the student can do.

Bill Phillips, Eastern Kentucky University

Teaching the Flip: Facilitating a Professional Learning Community

During the fall semester of 2014, I facilitated a Professional Learning Community (PLC) about flipping the classroom at Eastern Kentucky University. We started with 23 interested faculty, but because of time conflicts and workload issues, the group fell to 8-10 core faculty. Facilitating a PLC with faculty as members is challenging for several reasons. One, because they are experts in pedagogy, that aspect of the PLC has to be carefully and thoughtfully planned. Two, they are typically overburdened, so minimizing the workload on any particular member is important. Three, faculty demand practical tips they can implement right away. I sought to address all of these demands. The good news is that faculty also generally want to improve the quality of their instruction, and given the time and resources to do so, they take to it with zeal.

The PLC members had varied experience with flipping, but they all had experience with the elements required to flip a class. A flipped class has two general features: content that students access outside of class time and content they engage with during class time. Some PLC members knew about how to create content for outside the class; some knew about productive activities for in class. Thus, I provided a list of potential topics to discuss, divided into in-class and outside-class topics. I asked them to select a topic they knew something about from the list and present on that topic to the PLC. This strategy divided the labor among the members, meaning that each member would only have to prepare for the PLC meetings once, and the rest of the time that member could just show up with no preparation required.

Here is a list of the topics that faculty presented:

Delivering content outside of class:
- recording your lectures using PowerPoint, Prezi, and screencasting
- adding questions to videos (see Winslow, this volume)
- publisher ancillaries
- Google Blogger

Engaging students in class:
- wikis
- problem sets
- small group work
- jigsaw classrooms
- simulations
- student-created content
- inkshedding.

Each presenter introduced the topic and then described how she or he used it in classes. The focus was on the practical applications of the topics, and demonstrations were common.

Because the members wanted implementable tips, I encouraged presenters to email me their notes, examples, or instructions, and I then stored them on Google drive and shared the documents with the group. In fact, I used Google mail (Gmail), Contacts, Docs, Sheets, Calendar, and Forms to manage the content and communication for the PLC. The resources themselves were new information to many members, and combined with a presentation about Google Blogger by one of the PLC members, we demonstrated the utility of the Google universe for education. Typically, I sent out an email announcing the topics for each week and then another email summarizing what we covered in each meeting, with links to relevant documents. I was also intent on including the faculty who were not able to attend the specific PLC meetings, and using Gmail and Google drive allowed me to do this.

No formal evaluation of the PLC was performed. However, many of the absent members thanked me for communicating with them and keeping them in the group, if only virtually. I also discovered that several scholarship-of-teaching-and-learning (SOTL) teams were created among the members, resulting in at least two presentations at teaching conferences and the promise of publications. In addition, several members of the Flipping PLC signed up for the next semester's PLC (about metacognition) that I will again facilitate. I take that as evidence of the PLC's success.

Matthew P. Winslow, Eastern Kentucky University

II. Pre-/Post-Class (Out-of-Class Assignments)

You've decided to flip your classroom. Now, what do you do? This section highlights pre- and post-class assignments, also known as "out of class" assignments. While managing the workload of a traditional, in-class experience might be familiar to you, we realize that planning out-of-class work that engages students might seem new. You might not realize that it also takes a great deal of planning before you meet your students each day. Instructors must decide how, why, and in what ways they will facilitate learning that takes place for students, in the home, at work, or in a local coffee shop. That is, you must consider how you'll enable student learning through out-of-class readings, projects, and viewings.

Focusing on the pre- and post-class assignments, these tips encourage you to think beyond the walls of the classroom. Designing videos for use in an online module, for example, can present unique challenges, even for veteran instructors. You will likely need to learn about the basics of creating and editing a short video. In addition, if you're designing a web-based module, you will likely need to understand ways to make your content—whether through PowerPoint slides or Camtasia—interactive.

Reading Preview Clips

For some years now, I have become increasingly aware that many of my students have not yet acquired a knack for self-reflective and efficient reading. Many students will conscientiously dive into the assigned pages, but they perceive it as a wholly linear task to be performed once and without reflection. Under this approach, each sentence on each page assigned carries nearly equal weight, proceeding through the student's mind about as evenly as the letters from A to Z. Not surprisingly, notes made by such a student then tend to reveal a lack of awareness of the reading's overall structure and, thus, of the author's intended points of emphasis. The student simply misses most of the forest for the trees.

Having made this observation, I have wished to myself on numerous occasions that I could sit down with each student individually just before s/he begins the assigned reading to offer pointers of how to approach those particular pages. Although important, the last five minutes of class are simply inadequate to the task, not only because of the necessity of brevity, but also because too much time elapses between my parting comments and the moment students begin to read. I realized recently, however, that I could address this problem by providing students with regular reading preview webcasts that they could view whenever they are ready to open their books.

Thus, I decided to partially flip my class. For this purpose I created PowerPoint presentations that I then narrated on camera using the application Screencast-O-Matic, but any comparable webcasting software will serve, such as Camtasia Studio or Jing.

As I began making and posting my reading preview clips, I discovered that they served multiple functions in my flipped classroom, some more anticipated than others:

- **Structural Guidance:** As the reading preview clips offer an initial walk-through of the pages assigned, students gain a better sense of the interrelationship of issues, making them less prone to take a purely linear unreflective approach to the reading.
- **Calibration of Reading**: In the video format, I can give students very precise tips concerning which sections of the reading they should engage most carefully and which other sections they should simply read for the main ideas. (See, for example, my reading preview clip on "Europe at the Apex of World Power, 1890-1914," https://www.youtube.com/watch?v=puY7wPQ1MZs)
- **Questions in Advance**: For each section of the reading that I sketch, I also pose questions for students to consider. The students know that most of these questions will crop up in class, and they are correspondingly readier to answer them promptly, having had plenty of time to mull them over in private.
- **Elaboration:** Where I feel that I can make an important point more vividly and

thus memorably than does the text, or if I otherwise feel that the point requires reinforcement, I have used the reading preview to elaborate or illustrate in ways that I might not have a chance to utilize in the classroom. (See, for example, my discussion of the crimes of King Leopold II of Belgium against the people of the Congo, an issue that was acknowledged but sorely understated in the textbook. This discussion may be found at 15:46 in my reading preview clip on "European Imperialism in Africa, 1884-1914," https://www.youtube.com/watch?v=_NXiCt_2CFE&feature=youtu.be&hd=1)

- **Rectification:** Walking students through a given reading assignment has also given me an opportunity to comment in advance on the occasional relevant omission, ambiguity or inaccuracy in a text. Where the omission is significant enough for comment, I have also used the video for a mini-lecture on the point, explaining not only the facts, but also the issue's importance.

Overall, I have found that the reading preview clips contribute significantly to a positive classroom experience. Because students have a clearer idea from the preview clips why they are reading the pages assigned and what questions I am likely to ask later in class, they respond both more quickly and more fully when the time comes. At the same time, as the reading preview clips allow me to discuss a number of important points in advance, they alleviate much of the "coverage pressure" I might otherwise experience in the classroom. Students promptly pick up on allusions to issues I have already explored on camera, and I am thus able to move the discussion to the next level of analysis for deeper learning. As a result of these two developments, classroom interaction has increased in both quality and quantity wherever I have applied this technique.

John Lowry, Eastern Kentucky University

Extending My Classroom Beyond the Classroom Walls with Website Videos

After teaching in the primary for nearly eleven years, I was asked to teach 5th and 6th grade Language Arts and On Demand Writing. As super excited for the opportunity as I was, I was more shocked to discover how fast-paced and rigorous the schedule was. I left a self- contained classroom of twenty-six students to teach one-hundred-and-forty seven students daily! Time was of the essence as I had each of the five classes only fifty-five minutes per day. How was I going to successfully deliver instruction, have classroom activities, and still have time for independent work in this short amount of time? After careful thought, I decided flipping my classroom could solve those problems.

After strategic planning, I decided to make use of our existing classroom website. Nervously, I sat before the camera that afternoon and videoed my first lecture. I uploaded the videos, and watched myself deliver the lecture and instruction about writing an argumentative speech for sixth-grade students and writing a persuasive article for fifth-grade students. Feeling satisfied, I retired for the night with high hopes for the following day.

After explaining the process of flipping our classroom, I was inspired by the students' responses and overall attitude. I explained the process to each class. They would be required to log into the classroom website nightly, watch the video, write a brief blurb on their blog, answer the exit slip, and be prepared for class the next day. Writing the blurb and answering the simple exit slip ensured students' accountability. Each class was receptive and full of questions, but equally as excited about watching the lecture at home and having more time during class for activities and independent work.

Nervously, I checked the website for logins that night. I was overwhelmed with the number of students who were logging in and who had already posted blurbs to their blogs. Of course, some students who normally struggled with getting their work done during the day did not log in. I planned to deal with those students the following day by requiring them to log in during class time while the other students worked on their group activities.

The next morning as students entered the classroom, they posted their assigned bell ringer from the night before in the allotted classroom parking lot. In a matter of minutes the parking lot was full. I was thrilled at how well students were prepared and ready to work. The in class activities went very well. Students worked in their assigned groups of six, sharing their ideas of how to incorporate the necessary vocabulary into their writing assignments as well as preparing their first drafts. I monitored and observed students working collaboratively, supporting peers who had questions, while also observing students working independently. I observed the students who were watching the video from the night before on classroom computers working equally hard. During the final fifteen minutes of class, each group shared their findings and progress. As each class left, a wonderful feeling of accomplishment filled the room. I was ecstatic with the amount of work that was completed by every student in every class.

In upcoming days flipping my classroom allowed students to complete necessary timed writings to better prepare them for the rigorous timed writing assessment on KPREP. I also created an incentive to keep morale high and encourage students to continue logging in nightly. I created "Tiger Bucks" that students could earn for logging in and completing assignments for a specified number of nights and could be exchanged for various academic treats, such as drop the lowest grade, fifteen extra minutes in the class library, homework passes, five points added to the lowest grade, five minutes extra study time, etc. The incentives encouraged students to continue logging in, kept morale high, and encouraged those who did not log in to complete their nightly assignments as well.

I encountered very few problems with flipping my classroom, none of which were major or time-consuming to solve. Students also displayed an amazing level of maturity and worked diligently to complete their nightly assignments. This strategy allowed students to hear a complete lecture, listen to detailed instruction, and be prepared for class the following day via video from home. Not only were the students receptive, the parents were as well. Flipping the classroom was a great experience for me at the elementary level. I have since used this method of flipping the classroom in my college classes, where it has been equally as successful. I am confident this video strategy can be implemented and be successful at any grade level.

Joyce Ellen Bowling, University of the Cumberlands

A Multi-Modal Approach to Grammar and Punctuation within a Cultural Setting

A multi-cultural class brings with it a rich blend of cultures, and one student group that can often be present in such a class is the first-generation Americans who still have strong ties to their homeland. Many of these students are curious about the places and faces that are connected with their culture (Zane & Mak, 2003). However, it is not just the first-generation Americans who fall into this multi-ethnic category; many Native American students also have strong ties to their cultural heritage (Swisher and Deyhle, 1987). Then there are the Asian American students who have established family values that place a high priority on identity (Kim, Atkinson, & Yang, 1999); these bilingual students appreciate their cultural identity being celebrated with their classmates. Many Hispanics bring their culture into the classroom because it is a dominate part of their private life outside of the classroom (Gonyea, 2010). Also, the African American community has a strong cultural pride that needs to be valued within the learning process (Diepeveen, 1986). Since this cultural influence is a part of a multi-ethnic class, it would be prudent for a teacher to consider the value of a flipped classroom that allows these multi-ethnic students to experience a cultural connection in the material being investigated before the students even enter the face-to-face classroom.

Instructors who teach bidialectal or bilingual minority learners need to develop a pedagogy with culturally sensitive components in order to promote student agency (Gay, 2002). In other words, when you are teaching grammar and punctuation, incorporating cultural elements that will engage all your students is beneficial. Not only should there be cultural elements, but research has demonstrated that a multi-modal rather than a text based approach is often helpful for this group of minority students (Westby & Inglebred, 2012). So, with a flipped classroom that uses an online component, make sure the course also has an ethnic component.

First Generation Students

A first generation student will value projects that are tied to their homeland. First, have the student watch a video capture of you, the instructor, in the classroom, giving the instructions, while demonstrating the proper punctuation of a sentence on the white board. Then, provide these students with some sentences that they need to punctuate or correct, but make sure the content of those sentences includes cultural elements that will connect with the specific cultures represented in the class.

Native American Students

If there are some bilingual Native American students in your class, they might appreciate a PowerPoint presentation with voiceover that incorporates pictures from their community. Following each picture, have a slide with a grammar rule and sentence example. The sentence should be tied to the previous picture. This approach will allow the bilingual Native Americans the opportunity to see visuals that are connected to the text, while hearing the voice of the instructor provide instruction concerning the punctuation rules.

Asian American Students

The Asian American students might appreciate the chance to watch a YouTube video that reflects an aspect of their culture. Then, have these students write a paragraph summary of the video before they come to class. However, make sure you include specific grammar and punctuation details that should be incorporated into the paragraph. For example, the instructions could say: include three compound sentences, two semi-colons, and two apostrophes. This kind of assignment allows the Asian American bilingual students the opportunity to celebrate their culture while practicing grammar. In class, these paragraphs can be shared.

Hispanic Students

If you have a punctuation lesson to teach to Hispanic bilingual students, before class ask them to go online to find images connected with their culture, and have them bring those images to class. Also, before class, have them write a sentence about the image, but ask them to incorporate into the sentence at least one grammatical error. In class, you can have the students exchange the images and error filled sentences. The students will have an opportunity to see the images and correct the errors in the sentences.

African American Students

When I was in Africa, I used my iPad to record different grammar and punctuation lessons, while highlighting different cultural aspects of Morogoro, Tanzania. Then I uploaded these to YouTube. If you would like to see one of these videos, search YouTube for "Commas Taught in Africa." This video, along with other Africa punctuation videos, is watched by my students before they come to class. The cultural aspect captures their interest, the visual and verbal elements help with comprehension, and the lesson itself provides information that will be discussed in class. I have the students watch the comma lesson before one class, the semi-colon lesson before another class, the quotation mark lesson before another class, etc. This way they learn more about Africa while gaining some basic understanding about the punctuation element that will be taught in class.

It is time that the instructor of a multi-ethnic flipped class consider a cultural approach to teaching grammar so that the student's culture is valued and the learning styles connected with his or her culture are integrated into the learning process.

References

Diepeveen, L. (1986). Folktales in the Harlem Renaissance. *American Literature, 58*(1), p. 64-81.

Kim, B.S., Atkinson, D.R., & Yang, P.H. (1999). The Asian values scale: Development, factor analysis, validation, and reliability. *Journal of Counseling Psychology, 46*, 342-352.

Gay, G. (2002). Preparing for culturally responsive teaching. *Journal of Teacher Education. 53*(106).

Gonyea, N.E. (2010). The impact of acculturation on Hispanic students' learning styles. *Journal of Hispanic Higher Education 9*(1), 73-81.

Swisher, K. & Deyhle, D. (1987) Styles of learning and learning of styles: Educational conflicts for American Indian/ Alaskan Native youth. *Journal of Multilingual and Multicultural Development 8(4),* 345-60.

Westby, C., & Inglebret, E. (2012). Native American and worldwide indigenous cultures. In D.E. Battle (Ed.) *Communication Disorders in Multicultural and International Populations* (76-101). St. Louis: Mosby.

Zane, N. & Mak, W. (2003). Major approaches to the measurement of acculturation among ethnic minority populations: A content analysis and an alternative empirical strategy. *Acculturation: Advances in Theory, Measurement and Applied Research.* 39-60.

Mary-Lynn Chambers, Elizabeth City State University

Research Reports

The flipped classroom provides an excellent way of preparing students for what they will have to accomplish in class. Here's an example.

Students choose a topic related to our subject that is narrow yet significant. They investigate and choose information about their topic from reliable sources: the source may be provided or sought out on their own. They design a single PowerPoint slide summarizing the most relevant information they have found, according to very specific guidelines (below), and post this slide to the appropriate discussion forum in Blackboard online by a strict deadline. They must not duplicate a previously posted topic. I assess the slides and put them together into a single presentation and re-post this hybrid to Blackboard, sometimes adding my own material. During class, students give a brief oral report relating their information, speaking extemporaneously from their seats, and responding to questions: tables are rearranged conversation style. Students receive immediate written feedback on both the slide and oral report, including oral communication skills, at the end of class. Multiple opportunities to practice these reports throughout the semester and across courses, have enabled students to develop stronger speaking and critical thinking skills, as can be shown from video-recordings of their final oral exams. Blackboard deadlines in between classes force students to develop stronger time management skills. This strategy, along with other assignment-based strategies, has replaced classroom lecturing in all of my courses.

Guidelines	Points possible	Points earned, notes
SLIDE: SUMMARIZE your topic: A brief <u>title</u> communicates the main idea, a narrow but salient aspect of the religion's history, beliefs, morals, or worship. No duplication.	1	

Four to five bullet points on slide communicate accurate details related to main idea. Draw information from the book and from independent research: --Be brief but informative. --Use correct English. --End points with periods. No duplication of content on previously posted slides.	5	
Image or brief clip on one of the slides: creative but relevant; not clip art; helps listeners to understand main idea or a detail. Caption fully describes the who, what, where, and when of the image.	2	
Caption fully describes the who, what, where, and when of the image.	2	
A Reference cites the textbook in a standard format with page numbers.	2	
A Reference cites the source/s of additional information with working link.	2	
A Reference cites the source of the image, including the artist/photographer and working link.	2	
Your Name on slide. (point off if not)		
REPORT You expand on the points in the slides by speaking extemporaneously: you may refer to notes but not read.	5	
You respond knowledgeably or reflectively to at least one question.	2	
DELIVERY Speaks clearly and slowly enough to be heard.	1	
Establishes & maintains eye contact with all participants in the room.	1	
*Speaks in complete sentences.	1	
Avoids fillers, such as "ah…", "you know"	1	
Total	27	

Joan Crist, Calumet College of St. Joseph

Turning Old PowerPoints into Interactive Camtasia Studio Presentations

Many instructors use PowerPoint in order to do presentations in the face-to-face portion of their flipped classes. However, this program has been used so much that students tend to expect PowerPoint presentations when their instructors stand up to do lectures in their classes. But the students of the 21st Century use various forms of technology, such as: cell phones, computers, and other hand-held devices. Selimoglu and Arsoy (2009) indicated that teaching with PowerPoint presentations enforces learning effectiveness by stimulating students' imagery systems. So today's instructors need to find ways to transform their PowerPoint presentations into Camtasia Studio presentations. Camtasia Studio is a software that is used to record the audio and/or video of a PowerPoint presentation that an instructor has completed based on the content of the course. Once created, these Camtasia Studio Presentations that began as PowerPoint slides are uploaded into an appropriate platform and used for the pre-class portion of the flipped classroom.

Instructors can record their picture so that students can connect the words with the face of their instructor. In Camtasia presentations, students are able to connect with their instructor as if they are sitting in a face-to-face classroom. Most videos are 5-7 minutes, but these small videos can be used in the classroom or sent out to students before a discussion starts on a certain topic. I have used Camtasia Studio many times in my online classes because students need to feel like they are getting the same treatment as students who are sitting in the face-to-face classroom. Also, certain complex topics cannot be explained through email; a Camtasia presentation can explain the content in a step-by-step format so that students will feel like the instructor made the video just for them. Videos are useful in the flipped classroom because technology is a part of the lives of our students . . . why shouldn't it be a part of the college classroom as well?

References

Selimoglu, S. K., & Arsoy, A. P. (2009). The Effect of PowerPoint Preferences of Students on Their Performance: A Research in Anadolu University. *Turkish Online Journal of Distance Education*, 10(1), 113–129.

Antoinette M. Davis, Eastern Kentucky University

Stories of the Journey: Using the Power of Story to Flip This Online Course

Every faculty member's dream is that all the students arrive in class having read the assigned materials, critically analyzed the content, synthesized major themes and noted unique outliers. Additionally, faculty would love that students are so excited about the course materials, they can barely contain their enthusiasm as evidenced by their robust conversations in class, insightful comments, and plans to use newly learned content in the real world. The question is – how do we facilitate this enthusiasm and depth and breadth of learning? What is the key that opens students to this level of active and interactive conversation?

We believe the key is "story." We offer an online, three-credit elective flipped course at the undergraduate level entitled Integrative Health. This course explores several integrative health practices and as such is suspect of being airy-fairy or hocus-pocus. In keeping with this preconceived notion of the new and novel, we created a class built around stories and drama. Our course is introduced to students through a narrated PowerPoint Presentation (PPP) entitled "Stories of the Journey." Within this PPP, the premise of being engaged within a story for the course duration is introduced, background information is provided (description of how this class is a story), the story foundation is set (introduction to Carper's language of knowing), the story characters are introduced (including students as the primary actors), a preview of the upcoming drama is given (how the assignments flow), and, most important, an expectation of a happy ending is predicted (where we are all forever changed).

Background information sets the stage by maintaining that interactions are positive, neutral, or negative and that every interaction, no matter how brief, is a complete story in itself. Stories are strengthened every time we repeat them, and stories can be changed. Our specific example is that our course is a journey into integrative health, this journey will be experienced and repeated as a story by ourselves and our students, and we will all be forever changed as a result.

Our story is based on a foundation called Barbara Carper's *Ways of Knowing* (1978). Carper proposes that information is categorized as empirical (Facts – What is it?), ethical (Is it moral and responsible?), personal knowing (What do I think or know? How can I use this info?), and aesthetics (How am I transformed? What story will I tell to others?).

The story characters include students and faculty. Everyone brings his/her perspectives, preconceived ideas, knowledge, experiences and family patterns to the class story. Students create unique stories individually and as a group as the class journeys together to learn about integrative health practices. Faculty members act as facilitators along the journey by providing guidance and direction as appropriate and sharing their unique stories.

The drama includes the weekly class assignments, all of which require students and faculty to present the facts, examine the ethics, apply personal knowing, and share aesthetical "ah ha" insights within the class journey. This drama is played out within the discussion board environment. Students are forewarned they may maintain or change their stories based on what they share within the drama of this class journey. Faculty's responsibility is to keep the drama going throughout the semester.

The second assignment (after the narrated PPP) is to listen to a parable story and discuss the story using Carper's language. The parable ties into the text materials assigned for that week. Students are reminded of stories from their youth, previous real life experiences, lessons learned the hard way and a time when they believed in magic and miracles. The facts are easy to discuss. The ethics are usually evident, and students clearly note their viewpoints. Students report what their initial impressions were and how they changed as they read the assignments and engaged in discussion with their peers.

Next, students read assigned chapters in the text and develop a story of these readings using an insights (I), resources (R), application (A) framework. (I)nsights discern the true nature of a situation, and grasp the inward or hidden essence of things. (R)esources are references in addition to the text that amplify or complement the themes or topics discussed. (A)pplication is a blog paragraph that summarizes examples from life experiences that captures how the text material is related to the students' real world. Students post their IRAs on the discussion board and push and pull on each other's postings. They provide references to support their stances and applaud each other's learning progress.

After participating in the online story, IRA discussion and other assigned YouTube videos, PPP and TED Talks, students write 2-page story snippet summaries (SSS) that are a synthesis of the parable story, assigned readings, online peer discussions, personal experiences, and other assigned podcasts, TED Talks, etc. Carper's language is used in writing the summaries and provides the continuing story drama.

The final story of the course is told as a synopsis of student interviews. Their last assignment is to interview a practitioner of integrative health, analyze their stories, synthesize the major themes and patterns, and report back to the class with a newly created story, complete with empirics, ethics, personal knowing, and aesthetics framing the drama.

As students pause to examine the drama of their journey somewhere around half way through the class, they share how they are being transformed by their learning, how surprised they are that they have learned as much from the parables and each other's stories as the text assignments. They share how they will integrate new ideas and larger perspectives in their personal and professional lives. Students who complete this course remember the stories: the parables, the course content and their peer's postings. They credit the power of story to communicate with others on a deep level. They note the enjoyment of all the stories of the journey and report the transformation in their knowledge (empirics), morals (ethics), perceptions (personal knowing), and, most importantly, their "ah ha" moments (aesthetics).

References

Carper, B.A. (1978). Fundamental patterns of knowing in nursing, *Advances in Nursing Science* **1**(1), 13–24.

Nancy Nightingale Gillespie, University of Saint Francis
David Johnson, University of Saint Francis

III. In-Class Assignments

Many readers, we realize, will have plenty of experience designing assignments for the traditional face-to-face classroom. This section asks you to consider the flipped classroom assignment. We suggest that you reconsider previous strategies for designing in-class assignments as you read the tips in this section. Flipped classrooms often look quite different from traditional, lecture-based classrooms, even during the time you spend with students on campus. In-class activities promote active learning, and assignments often create problem-based scenarios for students to consider and work through. In addition, these activities allow the instructor the opportunity to work side-by-side with students, discussing questions when they arise while allowing other students to learn and listen as well.

From service-learning opportunities to interactive and collaborative assignments, flipping the classroom demands a more intensive level of engagement with students than traditional classrooms, and the assignments must reflect the idea that students should be performing activities during class time that allow them to learn from you, the instructor, in addition to each other.

Now That I Flipped, What Do I Do with All This Class Time?

Most of us are fairly comfortable lecturing. We prepare our lectures and have a good sense of how much material can be covered in the time allotted. Lecturing is also safe as we have a good sense of what questions students might ask, so we are rarely caught unprepared. If class time is not to be spent on lecturing, though, how will the time be filled and what skills are needed to be successful?

By freeing up class time, teachers can create engaging learning experiences for their students around particular goals for the class session that are well tied to the course objectives. Faculty have been creating such learning experiences for decades, and a significant literature is available outlining the steps for these approaches and helping faculty identify the skills needed. Below, we provide a list of some common approaches that can be used in the flipped classroom:

- **Problem-based learning:** Problem-based learning is a type of instructional design that allows students to develop knowledge by working toward possible solutions to a problem. This strategy emphasizes learning that is self-directed and applied to a real-world scenario. Problem-based learning begins with an open-ended or "messy" real-world problem designed by the instructor.
  - When designing a problem, begin with the end in mind. Ask yourself, "What learning outcomes are to be acquired within this course topic?" This question will also inform your guidelines for evaluation of the project.
  - Utilize a contemporary issue to frame the problem, and include engaging details within a narrative. For example, if an instructor needs to cover the concept of concussions, create a problem focusing on adolescent head injuries in high-impact sports such as football or soccer or the health of players in the National Football League (NFL).
  - The instructor can also choose whether to present the problem all at once or in an unfolding delivery. An unfolding delivery may allow the instructor to simulate more congruence with real-world settings. In a problem-based learning clinical vignette, the instructor may present additional patient information while students are working on the problem to highlight how obtaining information from a patient can be non-linear, may come from

multiple sources, and is often incomplete upon first questioning. When working with the problem, students begin to identify what they know about the problem and what further information they need. At this stage, students identify resources to obtain further information and utilize critical thinking skills to identify a list of possible solutions to the problem. The last stage of the problem-based learning is the reflection and debriefing stage. Instructors determine what they want the students to share (i.e., process, solution, or both) during this stage and within what format the sharing should take place, such as formal presentation or classroom discussion.

- **Collaborative group projects:** Jigsaw classrooms have been shown to be an effective pedagogical technique in more traditional classrooms, and the essential elements of this tactic could be easily imported into a flipped class. For example, students may be assigned a particular task to complete in groups that helps them extend the foundational knowledge acquired outside of the classroom. Or, students could be assigned to jigsaw groups, with each member responsible for researching a particular topic outside of class then coming to class as the "expert" with the responsibility of teaching his or her content to group members.

- **Student-created content:** Students may use a technological medium such as Google Drive to collaboratively create a product based on the skills needed to be demonstrated for that particular class session. For example, students may develop a useful handout/flyer that clients can use to understand a psychological diagnosis in terms that can be understood by community members. By using the Google Drive, students can simultaneously edit one document promoting active engagement of all group members.

- **Reflecting on learning**: Posing engaging and thought-provoking questions at the beginning of class based on the content of the material learned outside of class offers an opportunity for students to reflect on their learning. Students may work in pairs or small groups to discuss their responses to such questions. Walking around to listen to how students respond as well as discussing responses as an entire class (if the size permits) provides an opportunity to assess how well students understood the material outside of class.
  - o Questions can be developed by either the instructor or the students. Having students develop questions that lead to critical thinking can be an excellent way to gauge their understanding of the reading. If you choose to have students develop questions,

you may consider providing extra credit to the student whose particular question is chosen as one of the discussion questions for the class, adding some extra incentive to develop excellent questions. As an added bonus, you can develop a repository of discussion questions for future semesters that are potentially more relevant to current students' lives than you may have been able to create.

Nathanael G. Mitchell, Spalding University
Amanda Wyrick, Berea College
Robin K. Morgan, Indiana University Southeast
Norah Chapman, Spalding University
Acknowledgement: Thanks to Dave Morgan, Ph.D. for his contributions to editing.

The Half-Flip: Flipping One Day per Week of a Tuesday-Thursday Class

I became interested in "flipping" after attending a workshop on flipping the classroom at our Center for Innovation in Teaching and Research at WIU. My main goals in designing a "flipped" classroom environment were to not only implement activities and strategies to make effective use of class time and engage students in learning relevant material, but also to make class time more interesting for both the students and the professor. I decided to begin the task of flipping a classroom by dedicating the Thursday class period of my Tuesday-Thursday classes, which met for one hour and fifteen minutes each, to a flipped classroom environment. The two courses I chose for this approach were undergraduate psychology courses, covering clinical or counseling topics that seemed well-suited for experiential, hands-on activities: Clinical Psychology, and Substance Abuse Ethics and Special Populations.

I first asked myself, "What would make for a more interesting and enjoyable classroom experience for everyone?" Also, teaching evaluation comments have included requests for more hands-on and interactive class activities. An area of focus for improving undergraduate psychology education according to American Psychological Association guidelines (APA; 2013) includes designing courses to increase small-group experiences and activities such as project-based learning. APA undergraduate psychology guidelines also recommend ensuring students are able to communicate to an audience, including interacting with others and dealing with questions and differing opinions.

Principles learned from my own clinical training also added to the desire for flipping my classrooms. As a clinical psychology intern within a medical school, I was taught that learning clinical skills occurs in discrete steps and differs greatly from merely memorizing information. Medical students and residents are taught "learn it, do it, and teach it to others." Students first learn the knowledge to perform a skill; then perform the skill under supervision; and finally, teach the skill to peers, often in a vertical format (upper-level students teaching beginning students). I tried to extend aspects of this process and APA recommendations to classroom teaching, including beginning to flip the classroom. I expected the "teach it to others" part to be relevant to clinical psychology and counseling courses and to prepare students for future work settings that may include case presentations and treatment teams.

Therefore, a partially flipped classroom was planned, requiring students collaborating in small groups to present activities and discussions to the rest of the class each Thursday. Students signed up during the first two weeks of class for one Thursday of the semester, as part of a small group of 2 to 3 students. Each group was responsible for covering class material pertaining to that week's topic, through activities such as group work, role playing, discussions or debates, case studies or video demonstrations, and article presentations. Student groups were reminded to be sure to read the textbook and be prepared to lead a discussion or activity with the class that covers and illustrates that week's assigned reading.

A list of several possible options (a partial but not exhaustive list) for this assigned task was given, which included but was not limited to the following:

- Presenting and discussing a published journal article or case study relevant to the current class topic
- Presenting lists of discussion questions to go over with the class, requiring students in class to break into groups or comment on questions individually
- Showing example videos or video clips that demonstrate principles relevant to the current topic and lead to class discussion
- Demonstrations or role playing of important concepts pertaining to current topic (i.e).
- Presenting a topic and assigning members of the class to a debate on this topic (particularly for controversial issues, such as an ethical dilemma)
- Creating and presenting a survey to class, then subsequently discussing the results (e.g., opinions on prescribing psychologists, assisted suicide, etc.)

- Combinations of the above or other activities or discussions approved by the professor.

Students came up with a number of successful small group activities and demonstrations that engaged the class and enhanced learning. For instance, in Clinical Psychology two students demonstrated systematic desensitization, a common clinical treatment for anxiety, as a psychological intervention with children by having the rest of the class create an example anxiety hierarchy for a child who is afraid of the dark (e.g., beginning with the child going to bed with a lamp on and the door open, culminating with complete darkness and the door closed at night). This group then took the class through a role play of progressive muscle relaxation, which is often used in combination with systematic desensitization, by playing soft music and reading a script instructing students how to relax different muscle groups. This activity subsequently led to discussion of the intervention, how it might differ for children versus adults, and other challenges that might come up for a clinician. Other examples of successful activities included a student group who demonstrated modules from a behavioral skills training group, such as mindfulness and distress tolerance; students presenting discussion questions and ethical dilemmas from clinical case scenarios; and a student group who took the class through a discussion of a real legal case of a psychologist who was involved in a lawsuit based on confidentiality violations.

Informal feedback over the semester indicated that some students enjoyed the flipped Thursdays while others did not like the idea of having to prepare for or participate in hands-on activities. Some students seemed uncomfortable with the more active classroom, and the change from passively listening to lectures while taking notes. Other student feedback included difficulty meeting up outside of class to prepare an activity as a group and that not everyone in the groups contributed equally.

Overall, I felt that the flipped classroom could be improved, but met my overall goals of engaging students and making class time more interesting, relevant, and effective. Other benefits, such as using one another as resources and getting to know classmates better, also seemed to be achieved. With IRB approval, more formal evaluation of student outcomes from flipped Thursday classed are planned in the future.

References

American Psychological Association (2013). *APA guidelines for the undergraduate psychology major: Version 2.0.* Retrieved from http://www.apa.org/ed/precollege/undergrad/index.aspx

Jonathan J. Hammersley, Western Illinois University

Class Notes Summary

For each in-class portion of my flipped class, I assign a small group of students to write a class summary in a specific format, which consists of the number of words, use of prose with the possible use of bullet points, and attachments that can include visual and/or audio elements. The students assigned to write class notes summaries (usually three) are expected to meet after class and consolidate their notes into one single document and send me the final version by a certain time and date (in my case, by noon of the following day).

I always include at least one sample in my syllabus of what I consider an excellent class note summary. This example allows the students to have a frame of reference. It is important to convey to the students that they should write the summary in a way that becomes clear for a student who was absent from the class. Therefore, each summary should provide all information missed, including announcements and other details.

Usually American students feel comfortable with this kind of assignment. They are used to working in teams, and through group discussion they can produce a more complete summary and address their doubts among themselves. In case of doubts about the topic, I allow them to contact me because my goal is to help them learn the material. My office hours are immediately after class.

This tool is more challenging for some international students, particularly Asian, not only due to the second language, but also cultural differences. Some international students tend not to be as used to working in groups; however, this approach is a learning opportunity for them.

When I receive the summary, I correct and grade it, taking into consideration criteria (something delineated in a posted rubric) that include the quality of the content as well as the format and correct use of the language. In this way, I have to correct only one summary and can post it online for the entire class. The summary then becomes part of the course documents.

This tool produces many benefits:

- It is a great learning reinforcement tool. The preparation part of the class through the flipped classroom is complemented by my lecture and moderated class discussion, and then reinforced by the class notes summary.
- Students who miss classes are able to review what was taught without having to come to office hours.
- It allows the students who prepared the summary to receive direct feedback from the instructor (and sometimes from other students) about their writing skills and ability to grasp the class material and summarize it.

- It provides the instructor with a measurement of class learning and his/her ability to convey the course material.
- The summaries are excellent review material for the students before an exam.
- Summaries help students learn the material from the perspective of other students.

This procedure allows students to be more engaged in class, focusing on class participation rather than taking notes. In my experience, this tool has been an eye opener. Writing summaries seemed at first to be a relatively simple task, and initially I was depressed by the low quality of the students' work. However, soon after my implementing the procedure in class, my assigning low grades for poor summaries and showing my corrections in a different color, the students realized the high standards for the class, and their improvement was exponential.

Ricardo Averbach, Miami University

Practical Simulations for Flipped Classrooms

One of the persistent questions in a flipped classroom is what to do with the class time, especially in disciplines which do not admit of much "homework." Discussion is one possible solution. Single complex problems can be talked about from numerous angles, and students can learn to think about social phenomena from the experience. Case studies and service learning can serve a similar purpose. However, the incorporation of simulations into the class experience can add variety to classroom and also highlight complex and long-reaching causal chains.

In my own field of political science, many interesting phenomena have multiple causes, and the full effect of a particular act may only be felt long after the fact or when another act occurs. To pick a reasonably simple case, local government land use laws have large effects on population and economic growth, but that growth happens years after the zoning codes are implemented, and all local laws are subject to changes at the state level.

Discussion and case studies can address this kind of complexity, but because the reading for the discussion or case must be done before class, by the time the discussion begins, the students have an idea of how the chain of events plays out – and, therefore, they have the ability to play the case study backwards. Knowing the ending, the students find the causal chain of events obvious. Real political actors, however, have no ability to predict each other's moves perfectly, or to know what other events might affect a political outcome. Simulations put students in the role of a political actor and force them to play the story forward with the same limited knowledge, therefore gaining experiential knowledge of how actors behave and breaking them out of the post-hoc omniscience their reading provided.

The simplest way to create a simulation is to obtain one that has already been made by a publisher or to convert a case study. However, creating a custom simulation need not be daunting, and it can be specific to the class.

Begin by deciding what causal relationships the students should experience in the simulation. In the example case, students should learn how to zone property in local governments and then how state laws can affect local land use. Then, decide what rules govern that relationship and what perspective students should have. Zoning laws are decided by legislation, itself affected by lobbying, elections, and state law. The other important decision concerns the perspective students take in the simulation. A simulation that demonstrates multiple perspectives – government, homeowners, developers, and businesses – will be different from one that seeks to emphasize just one perspective. Having all students part of one government will produce a different perspective than having students split across several jurisdictions.

Once the basic framework – causal relationship and desired perspective – is selected, it is time to write the scenario. Two approaches exist – the detailed approach and the general approach. In the detailed approach, everything is spelled out in the scenario. Students are given roles to play and goals to achieve. They might have points assigned based on achieving their individual goals. Detailed approaches can be a bit like a puzzle – students have to figure out how to combine their goals in order to win – but they can also be set up as deliberate zero-sum games if it is appropriate to the lesson. The instructor is likewise under tight controls, unable to modify the simulation as it goes. In the general approach, students are given latitude to decide their goals and perspectives, and the instructor is able to modify the rules as the simulation progresses. In a detailed scenario, students might be told that they desire more zoning for parks, but the instructor – playing the state – will require zoning for low-income housing in order to demonstrate state superiority. Contrawise, the students might simply be given options for zoning, and based on what they pick, the instructor can either facilitate it or block it as necessary to communicate the intended lesson.

If the scenario is detailed, the instructor's role might simply be to answer clarifying questions while the students work. In a more general simulation, though, the instructor is active in having the simulation respond to student actions and can role-play with the students. Perhaps the students want to lobby an elected official, played by the instructor. The important thing for the instructor is to keep the simulation moving forward. When students make their decisions, the instructor needs to tell them what happens next – either from the detailed scenario or from the instructor's knowledge of the phenomenon. Once students have done their lobbying and submitted their zoning ordinances, the instructor has to tell them whether the state accepted or declined the ordinance and why.

The simulation itself can be a useful learning tool by allowing students to empathize with the people whose role they fill. However, it can also be an opening for analytic and reflective deep thought. A reflection assignment or debriefing can integrate what they have read with the experience to provide deeper understanding. The simulation can also lead to a new simulation that picks up where the previous one left off. Students who selected quality of life amenities (parks) in the first simulation then had to address public anger with housing price increases (and the attached higher taxes) in the second. Students can see the long-term effect of their decisions and see how past decisions constrain future decisions, thus providing a broader view of the causation of the phenomenon.

Simulations can provide an active learning opportunity for students in a flipped class, allowing them to experience applications of their lessons and to work through complex causal phenomena that are difficult to quiz without the hindsight bias that a case study discussion might provide. Finally, simulations are not as daunting as they might appear if instructors keep their eyes on the causal relationship and desired perspective.

Matthew L. Howell, Eastern Kentucky University

Luck of the Draw

Having students engage with the material and learn from each other is excellent classroom pedagogy (Mason, Shuman & Cook, 2013; Berrett, 2012). But students aren't always very good at picking who they work with (Collins & Goyder, 2008); their best friend, teammate or boy/girlfriend may be whom they sit next to, but that doesn't mean they are going to get the most from the class activity by working with them. Likewise, for faculty to choose and create functional working groups is challenging – getting to know many personalities quickly to create the groups takes quite a bit of effort. And playing mediator or parent is also no fun when a group becomes dysfunctional (Bacon, Stewart & Silver, 1999). In my flipped classroom, I have killed these two birds with one deck of playing cards.

Here is how it works: when my students come in, they take a playing card, the number of cards being equal to the number of students in the class. When it is time for collaborative work to begin, I determine how big the groups need to be for that activity and can easily sort them into groups of two (same color and rank), or four (same rank); or I can divide the class into larger sections, sorting by suit (four sections) or even color (two sections). Individual roles or tasks can be assigned (hearts are minute takers, spades are the reporters, etc.). I can rearrange quickly for a second activity during the same class. I have used this technique successfully in two different upper division (biology) courses of 10-30 students. To scale up, more than one deck of cards could be used, and the classroom could be divided into zones so students could more readily find their designated groups – two sides of an aisle are red or black, row numbers correspond to card rank. The groups are new and unique each class period, so students are continually interacting with each other, and no students are stuck with each other too long.

Not all students appreciate group work and having to teach themselves (see below)--nothing new when switching to the flipped style (Sams & Bergmann, 2013)--but this more random and arbitrary method for assigning temporary groups was anecdotally much better received than my dictating from on high with whom students work.

From my student surveys:

- Pairing up with different people helped with understanding the material.
- <u>No</u> group work.
- Sometimes I was paired with someone who didn't care.
- I liked it better when you lecture.
- Separating into groups in the middle of class was a little disruptive.
- Working with a random partner worked for me.
- Lecture is more comfortable for me.
- I liked that we always worked with different people.
- It seemed like you hardly lectured, the group work took up too much of class time.

References

Bacon, D.R., Stewart, K.A. and Silver, W.S. (1999). "Lessons from the Best and Worst Student Team Experiences: How a Teacher Can Make the Difference." *Journal of Management Education* 23(5), 467-88.

Berrett, D. (2012, February 19). "How 'Flipping' the Classroom Can Improve the Traditional Lecture." *The Chronicle of Higher Education.*

Collins, N. and Goyder, J. (2008). "Speed Dating: A Process of Forming Undergraduate Student Groups." *Eculture,* 1(1), 63-71.

Mason, G.S., Shuman, T.R, and Cook, K.E. (2013). "Comparing the Effectiveness of an Inverted Classroom to a Traditional Classroom in an Upper-division Engineering Course." *Institute of Electrical and Electronics Engineers Transactions on Education* 56(4), 430-35.

Sams, A, and Bergmann, J. (2013, March). "Flip Your Students' Learning." *Educational Leadership,* 16-20.

Karen E. Jackson, Jacksonville University

Using Evolving Case Studies to Deepen Student Learning

The use of case studies is common in many professional programs including counseling, nursing, physical therapy, and occupational therapy. A case study can provide students with "real word" problems to solve in the safety of a classroom. The effective use of case studies allows students to analyze, synthesis, and evaluate information to determine a course of action. Moreover, case studies can be created to introduce, reinforce, or master authentic tasks and skills students will encounter in the workforce.

The implementation of evolving case studies (Kiener, Ahuna, & Tinnesz, 2014) can be used as a means to flip classrooms and to increase student learning. Evolving case studies are used over multiple classes, and new information is systematically presented each class, requiring students to continually integrate new information and re-evaluate their treatment plan to ensure positive outcomes. Evolving case studies can also be used in multiple courses to increase the amount of information to be integrated. In addition, when students actively discuss the case study with classmates, the instructor can "see" students' thinking and assess for understanding.

During the flipped class period, students come prepared to present their treatment plan and discuss similarities and differences. The instructor's role is to facilitate discussion and probe students to think deeper about their plans. After the initial presentation and discussion of treatment plans, new information is given to the students and they are encouraged to evaluate how, if at all, their initial action plan needs to be modified. During the class period students are given time to discuss the new information with classmates, to gather data from the library and other sources, and to create a treatment plan that better resembles working with a real client.

In addition to students presenting their treatment plans individually, role playing can be incorporated into the flipped class period, requiring students to demonstrate both their analytic and therapeutic communications skills. Another way to use evolving case studies to increase authentic learning is to present the students with a client file instead of a traditional narrative case study. The client file can include numerous case notes, consent forms, assessments, and medical reports, all of which more accurately reflect employment and require students to demonstrate higher levels of analysis and synthesis skills to develop a comprehensive treatment plan.

With minimal planning, traditional case studies can be modified to become evolving case studies and used as an effective means to flip a classroom. Evolving case studies better mirror employment settings that are vibrant and continually changing.

Students who master content presented through evolving case studies may be able to demonstrate higher-level thinking required for employment.

References

Kiener, M. S., Ahuna, K. H., & Gray Tinnesz, C. (2014). Documenting critical thinking in a capstone course: Moving students toward a professional disposition. *Educational Action Research 22,* 109-121.

Michael Kiener, Maryville University of St. Louis

Building In-Class Activities through Group Work

Many college students have found themselves in classrooms where lecture is the main form of relaying information from instructors to students. Attending class and taking exams has become a part of mainstream classes everywhere. But it is essential for instructors to make in-class activities a part of their flipped class curriculum so that students can apply their learning to a project. Students need to be actively involved in the learning process, or they will be passive learners in our courses. Maiers (2008) found that when students are active participants in the learning process, they are interacting with the content, each other, and their instructor, and involved in conversations and decisions related to their learning. The 2010 NSSE *Annual Results Report* found that students who engaged in learning activities with their peers were more likely to participate in other effective educational practices.

In my classes, I have created activities that promote creativity and collaboration among students. Oftentimes, students are asked to work individually to complete a project. But I have found that students are able to benefit from the opinions of other students when they work together as a group. Group work is helpful because students can learn from the encouragement of other students in the course. In-class activities are essential because students can work together, and they have access to their instructor in the event that there are questions. Overall, these activities are needed in college so that students can begin to cultivate their learning over time. Without these activities, students will have to rely on instructors for critical parts of their learning. As college instructors, our responsibility is to teach students to be creative and active learners in our classes. In-class activities are the best way to place students in the driver seat of the educational process so that they can begin to navigate their own learning.

References

Maiers, A. (2008). 26 keys to student engagement. Retrieved from http://www.angelamaiers.com/2008/04/engagement-alph.html

Center for Postsecondary Research (2010). National survey of student engagement. Retrieved from http://nsse.iub.edu/html/survey_instruments.cfm?siFlag=yes&sy=2010

Antoinette M. Davis, Eastern Kentucky University

An Equal Opportunity Employer: Delegating Work Assignments to Collaborative Learners

In a flipped classroom, all learners must feel empowered to teach themselves. Each student should feel a valued part of the classroom community and be entrusted to take on authoritative roles in the creation, application, and dissemination of knowledge. One way to accomplish these goals is to distribute pre-assigned readings to students in small group settings with every member responsible for an assigned task. Examples of ascribed roles could include the following:

- **"The filterer"**: condenses large sums of information into digestible portions (isolating key ideas, highlighting important passages, and honing in on relevant discussion topics).
- **"The discussion leader"**: articulates information to group (rehashing concepts, posing questions, and/or employing creative strategies to stimulate interest and steer members toward focused conversation).
- **"The scribe"**: objectively collects and/or records commentary generated within the group (as a secretary would keep the minutes in a committee meeting) so that a chronicle of the discussion is preserved and can be played back for accuracy and clarity.
- **"The synthesizer"**: collates individual perspectives into collective statements and tries to ensure that everyone's voice is fairly and ethically represented.
- **"The spokesperson"**: communicates group findings to the larger class. Additionally, this person should offer insight into the behind-the-scenes process undertaken to reach the group's conclusions.

A more "expressivist" alternative to assigning work tasks is to allow group members to explore and define their own roles within the group dynamic in the form of "Debriefing Sessions".

How Debriefing Sessions Work:

Following collaborative discussions, each student is asked to do a follow-up response in which he/she evaluates his/her own contributions to the group discussion by 1) giving a creative title and 2) providing a definition for each role performed in the group's collective efforts. Example: The **"scientist"** of the group might be the person who continually tests the logical validity of the group's findings, while the **"humanitarian"** might be the person who is constantly questioning how the issue at hand affects the poor and powerless. The group's **"mediator"** might be the individual who points divisive opinions toward a middle ground, while the **"deviator"** always steers the topic toward an extreme position that is seemingly outside the scope of the issue at hand (but is still useful because it causes group members to "philosophize" about alternative approaches). As part of this reflection, students are asked to explain how the contributions of other group members helped lead them to articulations they could not otherwise have found, thereby enabling students to visualize their distinct place within the conversation.

Advantages of the Debriefing Session:

1. The use of "debriefing sessions" has greatly improved students' individual contributions to collaborative projects/group work, since they know they will be responsible not only for getting the work done but for being a unique "voice" within the conversation.

2. Having students articulate and define distinct "authorial identities" helps open up a related discussion about how these postures can assist them in solving tasks and developing fresh insights, thus expanding the repertoire of strategies and voices that are available to them as they read and write.

3. No matter what roles students perform in the course of the group discussion, a distinct correlation between how they perceive themselves outside the classroom and the authorial identities they assign themselves in the debriefing session exists (e.g., students who are generally more quiet and reserved are initially more hesitant about referring to themselves with titles that denote leadership or control, whereas students who are more outspoken see themselves as orchestrating the action but have difficulty envisioning how their silences equally contribute to the project). Unquestionably, nothing is more gratifying than observing students participate in "role reversal" as they learn that a time and season to exercise boldness as well as restraint are possible.

Cristy Hall, University of the Cumberlands

Individual Oral Presentations as an Alternative to Written Answers to Problems

So what kind of active learning assignments fill the flipped classroom in-class time? Here's one that demands pre-class work.

For many years, I have had my microbiology majors, most of whom are juniors or seniors, work through problems where they are expected to synthesize or apply course content. For example, with some problems students predict the outcome of an experiment that incorporates several topics we have covered in class. Problems are given a few weeks after the relevant material has been covered in class. This strategy allows time to provide formative assessment about the material, such as quizzes.

When I began using this exercise, students submitted written answers to the problems. In evaluating their papers, I always grappled with the perennial problem of not really knowing whether what I was reading reflected the student's understanding or that of classmates. Further, I just dreaded the grading. The class caps at 48, and a lot of papers had to be evaluated over the course of the semester. Several years ago, I began replacing the written submissions with individual oral presentations and will never go back.

Currently, the problems are given in sets of two. There are three sets during the semester for a total of six problems. Each problem, which has been provided beforehand, is discussed by the students over the course of a 50 minute class. Students are randomly assigned to groups of five to six to talk about the problem for 10 minutes. Then students are randomly assigned to new groups for a second 10 minute discussion. After this process has been repeated for a third time, the students are free to talk to whomever they wish.

Several days later, after working through the two problems that make up a set, students come to my office on an individual basis for an oral presentation. They have five minutes to convince me they understand the answer to one of the two problems (determined by coin toss). Students use two sheets for their presentation that they complete beforehand. One is provided with the problem and often takes the form of graphs or other representations of experimental data that they complete. The second sheet, prepared entirely by the students, contains supplemental diagrams to facilitate the presentation of their answer. The diagrams can be labeled, but no other written text can be included with the exception of a list of terms that must be in alphabetical order. These restrictions prevent the student from reading answers he or she has written out beforehand. They are encouraged to have well thought out supplemental diagrams that lead them through their presentation.

I have been very happy with this approach. There is no mistaking who does and does not understand the answer to the problem, especially when probing questions are asked. Students who have a good understanding of the answer rarely take the entire five minutes. Surprisingly, the correctness of the answers does not appear to be affected by nervousness although the least prepared students tend, unsurprisingly, to be more nervous. On a few occasions I have to stop students whose nerves are causing them to flounder and asked them to restart. The relative absence of discomfort amongst the students may reflect that I teach both lecture and lab in this class and have a significant amount of interaction with them before they come to my office. Consequently, I do think this approach would be more stressful if I taught only lecture and had limited interpersonal contact with the students.

That I remain stoic as the students are giving their presentations is important. Early on, I realized that my body language and comments were giving them clues about the quality of their answers. As students talk to each other, this telegraphing is an understandable problem to avoid. Ask probing questions especially when a student is not clear or rushes through is also useful. Students can come in with well-rehearsed answers that they may not necessarily fully understand.

More often than not, students come in with the correct answers. Where they differ is in the depth of their understanding and quality of their presentations. As of this writing, my future focus will be to help students better prepare their presentations using examples from past semesters.

Having students come to my office individually does take time. Although I have not done the calculation, I suspect that the time commitment for the three sets is not significantly greater than grading six written assignments for the class. Additionally, the students really have no choice but to truly understand the answer if they want a good grade. With the approach no hiding is possible.

Over the past few semesters, I've had students come back to back with five-minute gaps in between. From a time management perspective, this timing works well if you have other small tasks to do in your office to fill in the gaps (This hiatus is a great time to clear out your inbox). However, in the future I will be reducing the gaps between students so the presentations, as a whole, do not take as much time.

Most students show significant improvement with their answers by the third round. They come better prepared and go through their presentations more smoothly. I can think of a number of reasons this approach is valuable for students. However, in my mind, if they are even a little better prepared to handle the demands of a job interview, the whole exercise is worthwhile.

William Staddon, Eastern Kentucky University

Service Learning and Podcasting PSAs

By flipping my classroom so that reading, viewing, and other prep took place before class, I was able to use my class time to help my students create products—30-second PSA podcasts-- that demonstrated the students had actually learned something in their "homework."

Ernest Boyer's (1990) influential report on redefining academic scholarship has helped invigorate the effort among collegiate faculty to seek learning opportunities for their students outside of the classroom. Many valuable lessons can be learned by students who are placed in a situation where they are able to draw connections between the theories they learn about in their books and the practice they learn to implement in the outside world. In fact, Boyer warns us about what could happen if we don't strive to let students go beyond basic book learning: "If the nation's colleges and universities cannot help students see beyond themselves and better understand the interdependent nature of our world, each new generation's capacity to live responsibly will be dangerously diminished" (p. 77). The need to keep students connected to their environment has provided a significant opportunity for many professors to incorporate some kind of community service into their course projects.

In my radio broadcasting course, I was encouraged to require my students to complete projects that had a community service component. Scholars have made convincing arguments about how effective service projects and civic engagement activities are for undergraduates (Astin, Vogelgesang, Ikeda and Yee, 2000). Freeman and Rogers (2013) assert that encouraging students to become active in advocating for social causes "provides the potential for significant, long term impacts for participants and society alike" (p. 10). These kinds of pedagogical strategies fall under the category of service learning. As Britt (2012) indicates in her article, professors often like to implement service learning techniques that emphasize students' ability to learn new skill-sets while reflecting on the practical application they've implemented. She also points out that skills and abilities gleaned from the classroom become useful to students when they see that knowledge is relevant to real-world issues. In addition, Walker (2011) has shown that service learning strategies provide the opportunity for students to prepare themselves to participate in democracy and to increase their readiness for the world of work.

When one is teaching students media production skills, service learning can provide the opportunity for students to work with non-profit groups and community organizations in order to produce an appropriate media product, with an established target audience. Cohen and Kinsey's (1994) service learning study found that students showed increased motivation and contextual understanding of course material involving messages and audiences. Since media production requires a thorough understanding of messaging and audience, their study shows how promising service learning techniques can be for students in communication fields.

I implemented my service learning project in a course called Audio Production. The class focuses on teaching students the fundamentals of radio broadcasting, audio editing, writing, and on-line streaming. First, students were required to produce 30-second radio public service announcements. The assignment required them to identify an organization that had a message they wanted to deliver to a particular audience. Using what they had learned in class as "audio production specialists," students were then supposed to take that message and create a persuasive public service announcement that was suitable for the radio medium. (Students were also given extra-credit if the quality of their PSAs were good enough to run on the air of the campus radio station.) As they were completing this assignment, they became advocates of a community service initiative of their own choosing. In addition, they got to apply the production skills they were learning in the class while they were addressing the needs of local non-profit organizations. The specific skills they were applying included writing, audio editing, and vocal delivery. One student submitted his PSA to a national student competition and won a scholarship for coming in 3rd place. Some examples of PSAs submitted for the project include volunteering for community service activities, soliciting donations for non-profit fund-raising events, and informing the public about hazards or unhealthy habits.

Teaching media production courses also demands that students learn the best ways to distribute their product to their target audience. Since many of the students had projects targeting groups that engaged in a lot of on-line activity, a decision was made to create a class blog on WordPress. The blog included a series of podcasts featuring each student's PSA. Students learned about RSS feeds, Widgets, Managing Media Libraries, and strategies for Search Engine Optimization. By incorporating these PSAs into a podcast on a class blog, the students became promoters of these community service initiatives and advocates for the common good.

Overall, this project encouraged students to become more than producers. They became organizers. Their collaboration with others as well as their practical implementation of the course content during this process made students appreciate how transferable the skills they were learning in the class were to other contexts. One student who had a job working in the banking industry commented on how writing such a short script (only 75 words) helped him appreciate the value of writing short and succinct messages in a very persuasive way. Other students used the knowledge they learned about constructing a Wordpress blog to create a professional portfolio to showcase their work to potential employers during their job-search.

References

Astin, A., Vogelgesang, L., Ikeda, E., & Yee, J. (2000). *How service learning affects students.* Los Angeles, CA: University of California Press.

Boyer, E.L. (1990). *Scholarship reconsidered: Priorities of the professoriate.* Princeton, NJ: Carnegie Foundation for the Advancement of Teaching, c1990.

Britt, L.L. (2012). Why we use service learning: A report outlining a typology of three approaches to this form of communication pedagogy. *Communication Education,* 61(1), 80-88.

Cohen, J. & Kinsey, D.F. (1994). 'Doing good' and scholarship: A service-learning study. *Journalism Educator* 48 (4), 4-14.

Freeman, N.P., & Rogers, J.F. (2013). Fostering a climate of comprehensiveness: The pedagogical value of inclusive and service education. *The Forensic of Pi Kappa Delta,* 98, 1-16.

Walker, B. (2011). Developing an experiential-service learning approach in collegiate forensics. *National Forensics Journal,* 29(1), 6-33.

Eric K. Jones, Otterbein University

Community Service Learning and Collaboration in the Classroom Sustained by Flipping the Classroom

Community Service Learning (CSL) is a pedagogy to engage students in community service, focusing on the needs of local communities with the learning process. Students working in teams can serve a greater need that is connected with classroom learning outcomes. The goal is to combine the needs of the community with a plan for students to serve those needs in a manner in which classroom theoretical work becomes known to the students as relevant to a larger community. CSL has the effect of pushing the envelope to encourage application, analysis, and synthesis of theories so that students may experience learning on a different level outside of the classroom and in working with others (both fellow students and members of local communities or service agencies). Implementing a CSL component of a class is complicated in many institutions of learning due to the limited amount of classroom time that is dedicated to teaching specific subject matter.

Flipping the classroom can provide a sustainable means to meet traditional classroom objectives and outcomes and to provide a balanced means of reorganizing classroom time whereby students can collaborate and work in teams to address greater social issues in their community, bringing a CSL component to the classroom. Flipping some of the traditional in-class activities to the online environment allows the instructor to reorganize how time in the class and out of the class is utilized by students. Additionally, required static lessons can be converted for the online environment. For example, traditional class lectures and some teaching activities are easily reallocated as out-of-class activities. The in-class activities are then constructed to implement a CSL component to the class and/or collaborative activities.

Lectures are easily taped using PowerPoint 2013, saved as MP4 videos, and uploaded to a class website. To ensure that students learn the material, a pre-test/post-test quiz can be added. Students can be assigned these activities for outside of the classroom, allowing for the classroom time to be dedicated to creating teams, brainstorming among students, and collaborative activities to participate, design, or join a service project. In my classes, students organize a community event to bring awareness about a social issue such as community obesity issues, the needs of families of veterans, or environmental justice issues. Other ways to bring CSL to the classroom might be by partnering with other service organizations in the local community.

Collaboration for CSL many times initially requires some in-class time to successfully interact to build socially cohesive teams. In-class time dedicated to team organization, such as choosing roles for each team member and creating a team contract begins the process of student groups transforming into an effective team. The success and effectiveness of team Service Learning Projects are enhanced when the team is built using sound strategies to foster cohesion, trust, and commitment to the team goals. This process takes guided time in the classroom. The flipped classroom creates this time. Additionally, effective teams allow for less supervised or even unsupervised out-of-class team collaboration. Many teams fail to be successful because not enough time is used to create a foundation for that team. Once the students have created a socially cohesive team, CSL activities can then be re-allocated outside of class activities. Online components can be developed to help teams communicate, share work, and collaborate on deliverables for the in-class component.

When teams need some time to regroup, finish up projects, and present their work, once again, flipping the traditional lessons of the classroom to the online environment provides students an opportunity to report on their progress and allows the instructor to ensure that proper cognitive links are being met with CSL objectives and traditional in-class learning outcomes. Monitoring team work in this manner at various points in the project allows the instructor to give advice on how to keep on task, meet deadlines, operate effectively and efficiency, and meet the service component at desired levels. CSL and collaboration in the classroom can be sustained by "Flipping the Classroom."

Bibliography

Bowdon, M. A., Billig, S. H., & Holland, B. A. (2008). *Scholarship for Sustaining Service-Learning and Civic Engagement*. Charlotte, North Carolina: Information Age Publishing, Inc.

Rose, L. (2015). "Subversive Epistemologies in Constructing Time and Space in Virtual Environments: The Project of an Emancipatory Pedagogy." In *Critical Learning in Digital Networks* edited by Petar Jandric and Damir Boras. Springer: New York.

Rose, L. & Hibsman, T. (2014). Lurking, Spying, and Policing: Practical Strategies to Enhancing Engagement and Collaboration in Virtual Group Work. *Association for University Regional Campuses of Ohio Journal*, vol. 20.

Rose, Lydia, (2012). "Social Networks, Online Technologies, and Virtual Learning: (Re)Structured Oppression and Hierarchies in Academia" in *Disruptive Technologies, Innovation, and Global Redesign: Emerging Implications* edited by N. Ekekwe and N. Islam. IGI Global Publishing.

Stanton, T. K., Giles, D. E., Jr., & Cruz, N. I. (1999). *Service-Learning: A Movement's Pioneers Reflect on its Origins, Practice, and Future*. San Francisco: Jossey-Bass Publishers.

Lydia Rose, Kent State University

Killing Multiple Birds with a Single Stone: Using the Flipped Classroom Structure to Go Beyond Course Content

Educators are using the flipped classroom structure to increase student engagement and ownership in learning. Basically, lecture material is put on the course's website (often as video or audio podcasts), and various assignments and group work are completed in class. Students become responsible for reviewing the lecture material at home because they are expected to use that lecture knowledge in the classroom for assignments and activities, and they can no longer simply sit in their chairs in class, becoming disengaged from the learning process.

I have taken the flipped classroom model and transformed my research methods and statistics in psychology courses to allow flexibility in the classroom. The course layout is simple: review on-line materials over a weekend, come to class for group practice problems, do an individual assignment during class (similar to a traditional homework assignment), do a group assignment over an original research article that matches concepts in the current chapter, repeat (see the appendix for examples). After two chapters, students take an in-class exam, and the process continues for the rest of the course. Ultimately, students review 16-18 hours of audio podcasts created with Audacity™, an hour of 5-minute video segments created with Jing™, and at least 13 original research articles beyond their usual textbook reading. Students learn the pattern quickly, and many indicate through course evaluations (up to 80% of those responding) and spontaneous comments in class (at least 2-3 per course) how this format aided their learning of the material and increased their engagement in the topic matter. For example, one student commented, "In my opinion I think all professors should use this method--it allows the student to learn the material almost twice; once on their own, and second in class if needed. It also allows for easy and convenient clarification since you are in the class with us when we do our work, so we can ask you questions there and not wait for an email or until the next class time."

Yet, what I have found most gratifying about doing this pedagogy is that I can design my activities and plans for a class period to go beyond the basic student learning objectives of the course. Granted, all of my assessments are designed to measure the student learning outcomes for the course. But I can also include other knowledge and skills I want my students to have when they leave my course and then incorporate those into it. Let me give a couple of examples of how "flipping class" allows me to do this.

First, students are required to read an original research article outside of class, discuss it together in class, and answer questions about the article that reflect the chapter concepts and basic critical thinking questions that make them evaluate the validity of the conclusions the authors make based on their results. All of these skills are important student learning outcomes for the course. Students are also, however, improving their oral and written communication skills during this type of assignment, as well as learning how to navigate differences of opinion in research and writing; I specifically point out to them how important this process is, as most research is done as a group endeavor, and I only use articles that have at least three authors contributing to highlight this point. Because I teach at a regional campus of an R1 university, I also choose articles that are written by the faculty doing research in the Psychology department at the "main" campus. My students will ultimately transition to that department for their bachelor's degree, so I use these articles as an opportunity for my students to find out what research is being done; this strategy allows them to identify a faculty member whose research lab they may want to work in once they transition to that campus. This assignment introduces them to the faculty they will have for future courses, letting them know what research they do and giving them a chance to see what research they can contribute to when they move on to their bachelor's degree work.

Another example involves evaluating and modifying research surveys. For the first course in the sequence, my students must collect survey data, do descriptive and correlational statistics on some of that data, and write the results in a formal APA-style research paper. We spend multiple class sessions reviewing and revising a survey to use for the research project. I select one survey that can easily be found on-line, and students move into groups to determine which questions are appropriate for the data we need for our study and which are not. Next we discuss as a class which items should stay and be reworded. We take time to talk about questions that may be leading or double-barreled and what could happen if we kept those types of questions in our survey. We go through multiple revisions in class so that every student has a chance to participate in the construction of the final survey we use. This hands-on survey construction and editing work is similar to what they will experience if they work in a lab where they use surveys while finishing their bachelor's degree. This skill can also aid them in their future careers, particularly those who have already decided to go into industrial/organizational psychology or human resources.

To accomplish these beyond-the-course-concept goals, I need considerable class time devoted to the activities that will allow my students to develop these skills. Asking students to get together in groups outside of class time to work on these is unreasonable, particularly for my students, who are more likely to be non-traditional students (parents, working 30 or more hours a week, etc.) who simply cannot fit that type of outside-the-classroom work into their schedules. They can, however, review the online lecture material at any point in the day, regardless of what their group members' schedules are. Saving class time for these activities and assignments allows students to relax a bit when it comes to scheduling and allows me to create learning experiences that go well beyond basic course learning outcomes.

Appendix: Example Assignments

Chapter 3: Scales of Measurement and Types of Measures

Valenzuela, J. M., McDowell, T., Cencula, L., Hoyt, L., & Mitchell, M. J. (2013). ¡Hazlo Bien! A participatory needs assessment and recommendations for health promotion in growing Latino communities. *American Journal of Health Promotion, 27,* 339-346. Doi: 10.4278/ajhp.101110-QUAL-366

1. What was the overall purpose of this study? What makes it different from other literature on this topic? Note: Do NOT just copy the statement listed for the purpose that is in the abstract. Put this in your own words as a group.

2. Describe at least 5 questions that were used in the survey the authors used for this study. Make sure to list what the possible responses could be for each question you list.

3. Go back to the 5 questions you listed in #2. What scale of measurement would be used for each of the 5 questions? Why? (In other words, for your first question listed, what scale of measurement is that and why is that the case?)

4. For each of the 5 questions you have listed in #2, what were the general results that went with those? (In other words, what were the basic results for the first question you have listed?)

5. Imagine you work for a non-profit organization that specializes in helping communities become educated on health care concerns. Based on what you learned from this article, what are 3 things you would do to try to address the health status and care availability for the Latino community of Norwood?

Chapter 4: Descriptive Methods

Please answer the following questions as completely as possible, based on the Chapter 4 PowerPoints, Podcasts, and Reading from the textbook. Write your answers on notebook paper, or type them at the Computer Concourse and print them. This assignment is due at the end of class.

Set-up: You are currently working with a researcher who studies the development of racial belief systems in college students. You have been asked to develop a series of descriptive research studies to look at this topic in more detail. (Again, you don't have to be an expert on this topic – the focus is on how you answer the questions based on the content of the chapter at hand).

1) Describe how you would study this topic through naturalistic observation. Will this be disguised or undisguised observation, non-participant or participant observation? Be specific as to how this will happen in your study. What are the pros and cons of this format?

2) Describe how you would study this topic through a focus group interview. Be specific. What would be the pros and cons of this format?

3) Develop a set of 5 open-ended questions you would use for a survey method for this topic and write them down. What makes these open-ended questions?

4) Develop a set of 5 close-ended questions you would use for a survey method for this topic and write them down. What makes them close-ended questions?

5) The researcher you are working with reviews your survey questions and tells you that they are both loaded and leading questions. What does this mean? Be specific.

Sarah Cummins-Sebree, University of Cincinnati Blue Ash

Teaching Practical Grammar in Foreign Language Studies

This tip can be useful for teaching English as a Second Language to international students participating in Intensive English Language and Bridge Programs who will later pursue undergraduate and graduate degrees at American universities as well as for teaching a foreign language to college-level American students.

Mastering grammar is essential for second/foreign language acquisition; therefore, it takes a central part in foreign language instruction. Traditionally, an instructor explains grammar rules to students, provides examples, and checks for understanding. PowerPoints, tables, and charts are widely used as visual tools. After the explanation, students practice using the language structures in exercises, drills, and finally use the target structures for written and oral communication. Traditionally, explanation is done in a classroom, while most of the practical application is assigned for homework.

I suggest flipping the activities and assigning grammar rules comprehension for homework while spending the class period practicing the usage of target language structures. As many other flipped classroom activities, this one will help to motivate students, stimulate their learning and facilitate acquisition of necessary language and study skills.

One of the benefits of studying grammar rules independently ahead of practicing them in class is a different amount of time students will allocate to internalizing them. If needed, they will be able to return to the parts of a grammar rule they haven't understood, will be able to reread it, watch a part of the video with the explanation again, or email a teacher or a classmate for clarifications.

Flipping the classroom will also help to meet the needs of different types of learners. Audio learners will get a chance to watch a video clip on YouTube or read out loud the grammar rule for better understanding; visual learners will study the charts, diagrams and watch a PowerPoint; and kinesthetic learners can act out the part of the grammar rule they are going to teach to their classmates. During the practice class-time, students will feel more confident, better prepared and more willing to participate in language production and take risks. Their anxiety barrier will be lower, which will result in better communication and language retention. A teacher in this case is a consultant and a coach, who helps students use grammar structures correctly, encourages participation, corrects mistakes when necessary, defines strategies for students to improve their language skills, monitors their success, assesses the structure mastery, and suggests ways for improvement.

Here's an example of how the process works. Students divide a grammar rule, where each student prepares to teach a part of it using his/her own illustrating sentences and then teaches it to the rest of the group. Other group members have to summarize a student's presentation and answer comprehension questions. All of the students will be familiar with the grammar rule already, so the presentation only recaps the information students should already have. After that, students practice applying the grammar rules in activities, exercises, and situations.

During the second part of the class period, students do a project applying the learned principles and practices grammar structures with modeled situations. For example, if the grammar topic is *Degrees of Comparison of Adjectives* and the lexical unit is *Food*, at the end of the class period, students would work in groups to create their restaurant menus. The menu would have to include an appetizer, an entrée, a salad, and a choice of drinks. Later on, the groups share their menus with each other and create sentences to compare the items on the menu. Group A might say: Group A's salad is **cheaper than** Group B's, but Group C's looks **the most delicious**. Group C's soup is **spicier** than Group B's. Group C has **the most expensive** drinks on the menu.

This way of presenting grammar when teaching a foreign language helps to promote cooperation, academic curiosity, responsibility, and active and deep learning. This approach has been introduced by the author, discussed and widely supported by TESOL and foreign language teachers throughout the world at the International TESOL Convention in Portland, Oregon, in 2014 and the International Conference of Language, Literature and Linguistics in Phuket, Thailand, 2014.

Olga Filatova, Miami University

Flipping Definitions of Terrorism

Every semester I teach a flipped course on Terrorism and Counterterrorism, and each time the content changes slightly due to the current threat du jour. Fortunately, we can always begin at the beginning. The introduction to the course (as with most books on the topic) emphasizes the difficulties surrounding the search for a universally acceptable definition for terrorism. These difficulties are primarily political in nature and exist across time and space. Arguments exist for the absolute necessity of formulating such a definition as well as for the absolute futility of such attempts.

Students prepare for the first class by reading about these issues and arguments. Likewise, they are asked to view a few short videos that illustrate the complexities inherent within them. What, for example, is the defining characteristic of an act of terrorism? Is it the actor? This issue can lead to tautological thinking: terrorism consists of those actions carried out by terrorists, or terrorists are those who commit acts of terrorism.

Similarly, defining terrorism as acts of political violence perpetrated by non-state actors seems to leave out terrorist acts perpetrated by states.

These difficulties persist with regard to defining terrorism according to intent, or by target. Ultimately, most definitions when taken literally and applied objectively force us to include acts of political violence that we might feel uncomfortable labeling terrorism or, on the other hand, to exclude those that we believe to be definite examples of terrorism. In order to sufficiently drive this point home to students, the following group exercise (adapted from Bill Bigelow's "Whose Terrorism?" assignment from www.re-thinkingschools.org) has been useful.

After reviewing the aforementioned materials, students come to class prepared to discuss defining terrorism. They are placed in groups of 5-6 students and asked to come up with (or choose) a definition of terrorism that they can all agree upon. I generally stop by their groups and offer suggestions for consideration. For example, "Does your definition require harm to human life in order for an act to be labeled terrorism, or would the threat suffice? What about property damage, or the threat thereof?" or "Do targets need to be non-military in nature?" One student summed up this part of the assignment quite well by exclaiming loudly after the first 15 minutes, "I think we get the point! It's almost impossible for us to all agree on a definition!"

Eventually, however, due to time constraints, the groups slowly but surely come to a compromise. They are then handed scenarios that summarize events of politically motivated violence. An example would be something like this:

> The government of Akrum is very unhappy with the government of Nista, whose leaders came to power in a revolution that threw out the former Nista dictator. Akrum decides to overthrow the new leaders of Nista. They begin funding a guerrilla army that will attack Nista from another country next door. So Akrum builds army bases in the next-door country and allows the guerrilla army to use its bases. Almost all of the weapons and supplies of the guerrilla army are supplied by Akrum. The guerrillas generally try to avoid fighting the army of Nista. Instead, they attack clinics, schools, and cooperative farms. Sometimes they mine the roads. Many, many civilians are killed and maimed by the Akrum-supported guerrillas. The guerrillas raid into Nista and then retreat into the country next door, where Akrum has military bases.

The groups are asked to decide which actions, if any, in their scenarios would be considered terrorism by their definition. They must identify the terrorists as well as any state sponsors. In the scenario above, the guerrillas from Nista's neighboring country are always considered the terrorists with Akrum as their state sponsor. Students justify this choice by the targeting of civilians and civilian institutions in order to overthrow the government of Nista. Afterward, we discuss how these fictitious countries are actually pseudonyms for real countries and that these events really happened.

In the above scenario the state sponsor of terrorism turns out to be the United States. Nista represents Nicaragua and the Sandinista government, while the "next door country" signifies Costa Rica and Honduras and the Contras made infamous during the Iran-Contra scandal of the Reagan administration. Generally, the groups are unaware of this history and somewhat surprised to learn that their government would fund such activities. When asked if they would have been so quick to label these actions "terrorist" if they had known the true identities of the actors involved, they almost always say "no." "And that is why it is so difficult to come up with a definition that every nation will agree upon," I tell them. "Likewise, why it is important for us to study the concept that the CIA coined in response to Operation Ajax in 1953: blowback." But that's the next lesson.

Introducing the class with what could otherwise be a fairly dull exercise in semantics by allowing students to actively question the complexities of the core concept of the course creates an atmosphere ripe for critical thinking throughout the rest of the semester. Since questioning the taken-for-granted assumptions about politically motivated violence is a primary objective of the course, I must say that flipping this introductory lesson works for me.

Carl Root, Eastern Kentucky University

Flipping Creativity: How Pretotyping and Prototyping Facilitate Engaging Classroom Experiences

Tom and David Kelley recently published a book entitled *Creative Confidence: Unleashing the Creativity Within All of Us.* The premise of their book is that we are all creative (1). While faculty members often attempt to instill confidence in their students, who is responsible for instilling confidence in our faculty? Interestingly, their first chapter is entitled "Flip: From Design Thinking to Creative Confidence." This chapter will help you channel that creative confidence into your flipped classroom.

As we discussed in "Creativity and the Flipped Classroom," faculty might preference "creating" in the flip classroom environment to enhance deep learning (9). We emphasize this higher-order thinking in our face-to-face classes as well. The Noel Studio for Academic Creativity administers the Minor in Applied Creative Thinking. Courses in the minor focus on introducing the foundational concepts of applied creative thinking, innovation and creativity, the texts and technology of creativity, and research and creativity. In addition to teaching applied creative thinking, what do these courses have in common? They all follow a flipped approach. That is, they're flipped to a higher order (Sweet, Blythe, and Carpenter 7). Flipped creativity courses should create opportunities for project-based learning along with opportunities for collaboration and interaction between students and faculty. In the paragraphs that follow, I examine a set of practices that integrate applied creative thinking into the flipped classroom.

Flipping the Pretotype: Pretotyping is a strategy that often precedes prototyping (Savoia). During the pretotyping process, students create plans, rough sketches, conceptual maps, and other preliminary work to make determinations as to whether the concept has potential. Students might ask questions such as:

- Can the concept work if designed as a prototype?
- Now that we have a concept, do we have the materials to create a prototype?
- Who else might we need to involve in the design process?
- Where are the potential flaws in the design if we move forward on this path?
- Is there market potential, a need, or an audience for this thing?

The flipped classroom is the ideal environment for pretotyping to thrive. In-class time allows students to sketch and plan concepts with the instructor's feedback. Students then move the process online, digitizing the pretotypes using video or photographs, to encourage additional feedback beyond the walls of the classroom, answer questions about the concepts, or conduct readings or watch videos on design thinking as they consider the next phase: Prototyping.

Flipping the Prototype: The prototype phase often follows pretotyping. Prototyping entails designing a rough working draft of the project or artifact. Prototypes, as Tom Kelley and Jonathan Littman have explained in their shopping cart example in *The Art of Innovation*, often require collaboration, observation, and eventually thinking with your hands. During this phase, students might ask questions such as:

- How does the prototype improve upon previous versions of the product, design, or process?
- How might we test the prototype to watch users interact with it?
- What materials are used to make this prototype, and are there other possible materials that would work better?
- How do we determine if the prototype has merit or requires further changes?
- Integrating the prototyping process into the flipped classroom extends the interactive, hands-on experience seen in these environments. Prototyping also connects in-class experiences with online lessons or assignments.

Pretotyping and prototyping--processes that encourage students to think ideas through with their hands--while commonly used in design schools across the world, can enhance the flipped classroom experience. Projects and approaches that extend face-to-face and online experience in the flipped classroom allow for a more connected and coherent experience for students while providing the challenge commonly associated with applied creative thinking and rigor of the college classroom.

Works Cited

Kelley, Tom, and David Kelley. *Creative Confidence: Unleashing the Creative Potential Within All of Us.* New York: William Collins, 2013.

Kelley, Tom, and Jonthan Littman. *The Art of Innovation: Lessons in Creativity From IDEO, America's Leading Design Firm.* New York: Currency, 2001.

Savoia, Alberto. "The Pretotyping Manifesto." YouTube. Accessed 31 Jan. 2015. https://www.youtube.com/watch?v=-t4AqxNekecY

Sweet, Charlie, Hal Blythe, and Rusty Carpenter. "Creativity and the Flipped Classroom." *National Teaching and Learning Forum.* 23.4 (May 2014): 7-9.

Russell Carpenter, Eastern Kentucky University

Use of the Flipped Classroom for a Super PAC Discussion/ Debate in a Political Science Course

Flipping the class depends on strongly aligning the pre-class materials and the in-class practices. One of the objectives in a fourth-year Political Science course was for the students to discuss/debate the role of Super PACs in the federal election finance system. Super PACs are a controversial topic at any time when discussing the funding of elections within the United States. At the Federal level, the Supreme Court has rendered a number of decisions on the economics of running for public office. The topic is one that most students have some knowledge about, but they typically don't have enough knowledge to discuss the topic in depth during class time. A study of the laws and regulations can become very complicated and confusing. Also, the abuses of Super PACs are numerous.

During a recent semester, I planned for a discussion/debate on the uses and abuses of Super PACs conducted by both major political parties. The first part of the assignment was for the students to visit two websites and develop arguments both in favor of and in opposition to Super PACs.

Assignment, part 1: On the course's Learning Management System, two sites were listed for the students to access. The first site that the students were to view was found on YouTube (www.youtube.com/watch?v=cet3NcNNSc48). This site details, from a comical point of view, the pros and cons of a Super PAC. The second site to which the students were directed offers a scholarly review of Super PACs. Students were also tasked with reading "Square Pegs: The Challenges for Existing Federal Campaign Finance Disclosure Laws in the Age of the Super PAC" by C.L. Bauerly and E.C. Hallstrom (2012), found on Google Scholar.

Assignment, part 2: This part of the assignment asked students to develop a simple note-taking system that described a Super PAC, the role of a Super PAC in the federal elections finance system, and the pros and cons of this role in the political system within the United States. They were asked to decide if they personally believed that Super PACs should continue to assist political candidates for a Federal Office.

One week later, during a regularly scheduled 75-minute class, the question was asked of the entire class, "Should the United States continue to use Super PACs as a means to fund elections?" The students were divided into two groups. One group was to defend the pro side of the question with the other group of students defending the con side of the question. Students were allowed ten minutes to confer with their group members and then present ten minutes of opening arguments. After the 20 minutes of opening remarks, any group member could ask someone on the opposing side any question that was pertinent to the discussion. The debate continued for 30 minutes. Then, one person from each group summarized the team's arguments.

The final step in the flipped classroom was a writing assignment. Each person had to decide, individually, his or her position on the topic and then write ideas about it in fifteen minutes. Their ideas were collected at the end of the writing time. The goal of the writing was not for me to grade a polished piece of writing but to examine the arguments that the students wrote to defend their positions.

The goal of this exercise was to discuss/debate the role of Super PACs in the federal election finance system. After doing the outside readings, participating in the debate, and completing the writing assignment, the students believed that they had an understanding of Super PACs, and I believed that the students had formulated ideas about a Super PAC that they could defend.

Joyce Armstrong, Old Dominion University

Flipping the Classroom with Video Game Making

Regardless of the course I teach, the majority of my students have a problem with classroom lectures. In reality, this situation shouldn't come as a surprise as the current state of our society promotes and premiums interactive communications. For college students to text message dozens of times per day, check a variety of social media sites multiple times every hour (Almeida, 2014), or generate content while in class isn't uncommon. The issue we are faced with is clear. How do we effectively educate a highly technological and pragmatic society with a 19th century classroom structure? The answer I found is with technology in a flipped classroom format.

For the past four years, I have flipped my classrooms, partly or totally. I've learned a number of important and necessary lessons ranging from the value that feedback (Mory, 2004) has on student learning to the disconnect and disinterest between traditional lecture and student response.

Flipping my classrooms has increased student attendance and participation. It has helped me to manage my classroom more effectively, resulting in higher student achievement, which has been quite exciting.

My most successful flipped classroom strategy has been building in-class activities that involve video game making. In my Communications Media 306 titled, "2D Digital Game Development," we build video games mostly during class time. The class follows a blend of constructionism (Papert, 1980) with a touch of behaviorism delivered in a one-on-one feedback format.

Students are required to either watch the chapter lesson on a webcast or do the chapter readings prior to class in order to take the quizzes, also on their own time. Class time, however, is spent discussing topics related to the book (the minority of time) and doing video game development (the vast majority of the time).

In the field of media, building in-class activities works very well, especially if the instructor spends part of his/her time going to students' stations one-on-one. My time and expertise have been well spent and received by the learners. In a period of a semester, a number of my students have developed commercial quality 2D video games for profit, an achievement that I've never seen in my career as a college professor.

Empowering the learners through user-design (Carr-Chellman, 2007) resulting in learning by doing (Schank, 1995) with in-class time dedicated to individualized student feedback (Mory, 2004) worked very well. I predict that it might even be part of how we reinvent education.

Flipping the classroom using in-class activities involving video game making worked wonders for me.

References

Almeida, L. (2014). The impact of computerized devices on undergraduate students behavior. International Journal of Instructional Technology and Distance Learning (1), 31-47.

Carr-Chellman, A. (2007). *User Design.* Sage Publications.

Mory, E. H. (2004). Feedback research review. In D. Jonassen (Ed.), Handbook of research on educational communications and technology (pp. 745–783). Mahwah, NJ: Erlbaum Associates.

Papert, S. (1980). Mindstorms. Children, Computers and Powerful Ideas. New York: Basic books.

Schank, Roger C. (1995) What We Learn When We Learn by Doing. (Technical Report No. 60). Northwestern University, Institute for Learning Sciences.

Luis Camillo Almeida, Indiana University of Pennsylvania

Flipped Classroom Student as Teacher: Merchandising Case Studies

Merchandising is big business and one that has taken on greater prominence with the rise of media in reality TV programming, such as *Project Runway*, *Say Yes to the Dress,* and *What Not to Wear*. Students are often so immersed in the entertainment value of media that they ignore the business behind the camera. Conversely, academic classes teaching concepts and terminology behind the three-trillion dollar industry can be somewhat dry. This flipped classroom aims to "meet the student where they are" through the use of varied media while also strengthening teamwork, presentation, and interpersonal skills, thus leveraging the student as teacher and the teacher as facilitator.

Desired Outcomes:
1. Gain competency in <u>time management</u> working with another student.
2. Identify, interpret, and <u>critique</u> marketing and merchandising strategies.
3. Prepare and present a compelling <u>presentation</u>.
4. Initiate and <u>lead</u> questions and discussion with the whole class.

This class of 20 meets once per week for two hours and 50 minutes over 15 weeks. This particular class is broken down into three distinct five-week segments. Courses where the subject matter builds are well suited for this flipped classroom. This flipped class could easily be modified for shorter class sessions.

At the start of the semester the teacher creates teams of two. Over the course of the 15 weeks, each student will be assigned two cases. For example, if there are three segments, students might be assigned segment one and two or segment one and three, but they will make two presentations over the 15 week semester. Additionally, the students will not be paired with the same team member twice. Students may not self-select. Teams are assigned the topic segment they will research and then present to the class. Below is an example of the presentation outline. Note that multiple teams are presenting over more than one week.

Week 3	John / Susan	Project One – Product Development
	Joe / Jeff	
Week 4	Mary / Heather	
	Beth / Natalie	
Week 5	Susan / Jeff	Project Two – Distribution / Store Layout
	John / Mallory	
Week 6	Lisa / Mary	
	Lauren / Carly	
Week 7	Joe / Mallory	Project Three – Promotional Plan
	Heather / Natalie	
	Beth / Jasmine	

The Process:

Students are given significant freedom on their presentations; however, they must discuss a minimum of two concepts from the project unit. Each project includes several sub-topics or concepts. For example, project one discussions may cover demographics, psychographics, product pricing, or fabrication among others. One team might select demographics and pricing while another demographics and psychographics. Although there may be overlap in topic, the teams find their own unique methods and voice in connecting the concepts, further strengthening students' understanding of the material.

Once the assignment is launched, students meet briefly with their partner in class to brainstorm which topics they might like to address. The learning begins outside the class and is then brought back into the class for student to become teacher and teacher to become facilitator. Student teams are charged with investigating their chosen topic by securing a minimum of two business articles or other media examples from trusted sources, which they combine to tell their story. Sources have included promotional YouTube videos from brands, retailers' own video or media commercials, business articles, and clips from television programming to demonstrate their understanding of the concepts while also placing them into real world context by example.

Presentations are derived from the above sources and then woven together to inform the student learning process as well as their own critical analysis. Most presentations last 15-20 minutes and are exhibited using Prezi or PowerPoint programs. The nature of mixing contemporary media with traditional sources becomes an inspiration for students in how they tell the story. What is most intriguing is the level of student engagement and retention of the material. Students interject, disagree, agree, ask questions, "lean in" and even forgot they are in class. As the presentations conclude, the team seeks input and feedback from the class. They lead the discussion about the key points to check for understanding with their classmates. At times the teacher will need to initiate dialog or probe for deeper understanding, but most often the discussion is raised to greater levels of inquiry about social justice, ethics, values, race, and more.

Breaking the class period down – 50% lesson and 50% flipped classroom:

- Arrival, attendance, returning homework (10)
- Recap from prior week and agenda for current class (10-15)
- Lesson for the day – often a game or small group activity that involves conversation and physical movement around the classroom. (30)
- Groups present from the lesson activity and the ideas or concepts are highlighted (20)
- Break (15)
- *Team Case Presentations (60)*
- *Instructor led presentation recap connecting the threads from all presentations (15-20)*
- Wrap up and next week's expectations (10)

Evaluation:

- Were they successful in conveying the concepts to the class for greater understanding.
- The level of creativity and sources used – were they linked and cohesive?
- What level is their own command of the concepts and ability to teach their classmates?
- How well have they worked as a team to present a unified idea from multiple sources?
- Overall presentation skills – verbal engagement and visual interest.

In most instances each team member earns the same grade; however, on occasion one presenter obviously lacks the depth of knowledge and may earn a lower grade.

In conclusion, flipping this classroom has made students responsible for their own learning on their terms and, at the same time, informs overall pedagogy for the teacher to learn from the student using current technology and media from contemporary society.

Pulling information from many students into one topic area brings forth diverse viewpoints through a variety of examples that might otherwise be lacking in creativity and interest from students. The success of this class is echoed by the students:

- "Before this class, I didn't understand what is merchandising and the steps it takes to get a product to the consumer. I've left the class understanding all the necessary steps it takes to sell a product in a store."
- "The delivery of the in-class material was extremely useful and taught effectively. For example, each student was paired with another student to give a presentation about two articles that reflected the particular project we were working on during that week of class. By correlating the presentation with the project helped put the project in real-life perspective. *Now, I feel more confident using the lessons from class.*"

Dana Connell, Columbia College Chicago

Flipping the Online Classroom

When I heard the term "flipped classroom" my first year teaching in higher education, I remember thinking, "What on earth is that?" It wasn't until after I attended a couple of sessions at education conferences where the topic focused on the flipped classroom that I realized I was already doing some of the things they were talking about in my own course. I teach online graduate courses that are made up of eight-week biterms. This schedule does not allow very much time for me to cover all of the content in great depth; therefore, I assign my students advanced readings so they can come to class prepared to discuss the content rather than my spending the entire time lecturing on something about which they may not have any background knowledge. This prior preparation allows time for meaningful in-class discussions about the topic as well as pulling in supplemental resources to further broaden their knowledge.

One specific teaching strategy I use that my candidates really seem to enjoy is what I refer to as an "online interactive quiz." I create a PowerPoint based on the assigned readings that consists of approximately ten multiple choice questions (one per slide). Blackboard provides an option to implement "polling." I change the polling options to A-D so that the candidates can click on what they believe to be the correct answer. Another option I can control makes their answers visible only to me. This option prevents students from seeing each other's responses so that they have to make a choice themselves instead of waiting to see what their peers choose. The first question is displayed on the white board, and the candidates are given one to two minutes to respond. Once time is up, I display the correct answer on the screen along with an explanation of *why* it is the correct answer and *where* the information can be located in their textbooks. This strategy has been a great way of breaking up the monotony of expecting them to sit and listen to me lecture each week. It also allows me to see who is actually reading the assignments and who is actively participating in class rather than just logging in and then tuning out!

Jennifer Chambers, University of the Cumberlands

IV. Electronic Resources

  You might wonder about the technological expertise needed to design, implement, and facilitate a flipped classroom. This section delves deeper into that important part of the flipped classroom development process. Like it or not, flipped classrooms are largely organized around electronic environments. Whether you're using a course-management system or simply directing students to an online video, the flipped classroom requires proficiency with technology.

  In this section, you'll read tips that will help you bridge the gap between your face-to-face and online classes. Tips reveal how you might use electronic resources to create coherence between your face-to-face classes and your online resources, which can be critical to your success as a flipped classroom instructor. One question that we always receive is: How can you engage students through video? Flipping your classroom means that you are delivering a significant amount of content outside of the classroom. Resources like Zaption, for example, will allow you to design more interactive and engaging online content. The tips in this section will show you how.

The Great Gap

Daniel Boone might have found it easier to trek through the Cumberland Gap than today's faculty explorers trying to cross the great digital divide. In Kentucky, this metaphor rings especially true, for no matter how much we as instructors believe in the effectiveness of the pedagogical theory known as the flipped classroom, actually trying this approach poses problems in terms of our students' access. More specifically, some areas of our university's 22-county service region does not possess the technological requirements necessary for the flipped classroom, either on ground or online, to function properly and fairly.

According to a recent article in the *Lexington Herald-Leader*, in terms of broadband availability in this country, Kentucky currently ranks 46th. Furthermore, while most of the state's rural areas have access to an Internet Service Provider, 23% of rural regions are not provided with broadband (A7)—that's one-quarter of the Commonwealth. Obviously, students in these negative pockets of access can't connect quickly nor can their carriers provide large amounts of information. One of our students mentioned that while he was attending high school in this area, access could be achieved only by driving to the local McDonald's. "Do you want fries with that download?" One commentator has suggested closing the gap by providing students who have problems with CDs or jump drives of the online materials, but such solutions place unreasonable demands in terms of time and money on faculty constructing out-of-class materials.

Even physical access can be a problem with commuting students. As one school superintendent explained, it snows a lot in the mountains, and when it does, the only snowplow is Mother Nature.

Finally, problems with digital and physical access bring up an ethical question. If any of our population cannot obtain access, is it fair to provide pedagogical approaches such as a flipped classroom?

We don't think these problems are unique to our university, but, even if they were, all schools have problems. For instance, at institutions where a four-course-per-semester load is *de rigueur*, is it asking too much to have already overworked faculty convert a class to the flipping format? Does the institution have sufficient resources (e.g., expertise, personpower, funding, technology, IT support) in terms of faculty development necessary to transform faculty into flippers? Does the flipping format actually demand more work from students? Are college seniors who are putting in an average of only five hours per week studying going to accept the increased workload that a flipped class demands?

In essence, every school has gaps to span.

Works Cited

Brammer, Jack. "Deal Made for Statewide High-Speed Internet." *Lexington Herald-Leader* 24 December 2014: A7. Print.

Charlie Sweet, Eastern Kentucky University
Hal Blythe, Eastern Kentucky University
Rusty Carpenter, Eastern Kentucky University

A Public Google Calendar for Coordinating Out-of-Class Content

Flipped classes, along with other active-learning pedagogies, depend heavily on organization and communication with students. How do we make sure that students know what material they are supposed to be accessing to prepare for a particular class meeting? No matter how detailed we make the schedule in the syllabus, some students don't read it; no matter how conscientious we are to mention reading assignments in class, some students missed that day, or didn't hear, or misheard. Also, we often can't predict before the semester starts what we will need to cover on a particular day. We may need to spend an extra day on difficult material, or go back and review content from a prerequisite course. There may be class cancellations to accomodate. Real schedules are messy, and if you create a revised schedule, you run the risk that a student may accidentally use the old version and prepare the wrong material for class.

Creating a Google Calendar for your class is an easy and effective way to coordinate out-of-class activities and to make sure your students know what they will be doing in a given class meeting. A majority of our students have grown up using mobile devices and computers to instantly answer any question they have by looking the answer up on some website. It is completely natural for them to answer the question "Hey, what are we doing in class Wednesday?" in the same way. Since Google Calendars are shared documents, changes to them happen in real time, eliminating the problem of old versions. Of course, students who use Google Calendar as their regular calendar software will have no trouble integrating the course calendar into their schedule, but by making the calendar public, it can be viewed by anyone with a web browser, averting the perennial difficulty with students who can't access Blackboard or Moodle. A URL shortener is a useful tool for making the address easy to remember or jot down on a whiteboard; we have had good results using TinyURL (http://www.tinyurl.com). For those who could use help setting up a calendar, Google has a page of instructionals for new users (https://support.google.com/calendar/).

When using this kind of "live" document for course control, avoid the impression that you are throwing assignments at the student at the last second. Block out the entire semester in advance in the same way as a syllabus schedule, but, as assignments approach,add more detail to entries. For instance, an entry that would simply read "Chapter 2.3, pp. 27-34" in a syllabus schedule would look the same on the Google Calendar, but when clicked reveals additional directions. "Focus on Figure 2.2. Why does the curve slowly increase from left to right but drop sharply when beginning a new row? Which has a higher first ionization energy, boron or carbon, and why?" This sort of detailed prompt allows the instructor to easily guide inexpert readers in the unstructured environment outside the classroom, preparing them for higher-level work inside the classroom.

Modern college students are sophisticated consumers of technology and are easily demoralized by instructional technology that works poorly, particularly in the challenging and possibly new environment of a flipped classroom. The shared public calendar is a simple and robust tool for directing out-of-class student work, making it easier for students to assume responsibility for their own preparation--a keystone of the flipped class.

Nicholas Marshall, Berea College

Engaging Students in Video Outside of Class

Flipping a class means that content is largely delivered outside of class time. While many manners (and media) can accomplish this goal, video offers several advantages. One, students are increasingly digital natives, so they are familiar with watching videos on computers or mobile devices. Two, rich and varied content already exists, created by textbook publishers, other instructors, students, and more. A Google search of a key word in nearly any field returns many options. Three, with screencasting software, simple-to-use video editing software, and presentation software such as PowerPoint or Prezi, instructors can create their own videos. These videos can then be uploaded to the web (using YouTube or Vimeo, for example). This way, instructors can tailor the content they wish students to access to fit their learning goals.

How can instructors engage students in the largely passive activity of watching a video and ensure that they access the content? Recently, a number of companies have developed software to address these concerns.

The solution to the problems of engagement and access provided by these programs is to embed interactive elements into the videos, engaging the passive student viewer during the video with questions (or other elements, see below) about the content and to record the students' responses, providing evidence of their access (and comprehension) of the content.

There are two methods for adding elements to videos. One is using web-site based software, and the other is using software; the other is on a computer. The web-site based software has several advantages, primarily that the user does not need to have a copy of the video on the computer; videos on the Internet like YouTube video or TED talks can be used. The computer-based method requires the video file itself.

The three web-based programs I review here are Zaption (www.zaption.com), eduCanon (www.educanon.com), and EDpuzzle (edpuzzle.com). All three websites offer free accounts for instructors and students, although Zaption and eduCanon also offer pay accounts ($80 – $89 per year) that provide more options for adding elements and better analytics and data downloads for instructors or campuses (a valuable feature, see below). The three websites use different terminology for the elements (elements, questions) and the finished products (tours, bulbs); however, the basic process of adding questions to videos is similar across platforms. Once the instructor has created an account on the site, she would either search for content using their web search tools, or paste in a link to an unlisted video (if she had created one on YouTube, for example). She would then have many options for the types of elements she could add to the video, including basic question types, such as multiple choice, true/false, and open response questions, but also more web-specific types, such as draw on the slide, check boxes, location-based maps, and even discussion. Adding elements is typically a matter of pausing the video where you want to add the element and dragging the type of element onto the video. The user interfaces vary but are designed for people without coding experience. Drag-and-drop is the norm. The websites vary in how they want students to access the videos. Zaption requires that students link directly to the videos, while eduCanon and EDpuzzle provide embed codes that can be added to websites or learning management system (LMS) like Blackboard.

The elements added to the videos engage the students in the material, while the data provided by the websites about students' responses offer evidence of student access and comprehension. The three websites vary significantly in the data they provide and the accessibility and usability of that data. Zaption provides data about average time spent watching the tour (video), number of skips forward and backward, and the number of viewers on each day. The other two websites focus more on whether the students provided or selected the correct response. All three sites offer data download with a premium account (CSV format) showing individual student performance, including responses to questions, viewing time, and date. At this point none of the services offers integration of the student data into LMS. This omission results in some tedious data entry if you want grades from the videos to display on a LMS.

The alternative to using one of the three websites mentioned above is to use Camtasia screen recording and editing software (http://www.techsmith.com/camtasia.html). While Camtasia is commonly used to create screen capture videos, it also has a quizzing feature that allows instructors to add questions to videos. This method requires the user to have a copy of the video file to import into (or create within) Camtasia. The other consideration with Camtasia is the price: single user licenses are $299, although education discounts lower that to $179. This amount is a big up-front cost, but once you consider that the websites' premium accounts cost about half as much each year, it is not so objectionable. The process of adding questions in Camtasia is similar to the three websites, if not quite so user-friendly. Not as many options for types of elements exist in Camtasia, and data is delivered via email. Camtasia claims to integrate with Blackboard, but I had trouble doing so working with my on-campus Blackboard expert.

The three websites and one software program described above help solve two problems faced by instructors wishing to flip their classes: how to engage students in (largely passive) video content, and how to be sure that students actually access and comprehend the content outside of class. The solution is to add questions (or other elements) to the videos, and to collect the students' responses to those questions. I have had success using Zaption and can vouch for its ease of use both for instructor and students, but the other websites seem just as easy and feature-rich. Adding quizzes in Camtasia is just one of a myriad of that software's features, so if you already use Camtasia for other purposes, using this feature seems like an easy option.

Matthew P. Winslow, Eastern Kentucky University

TED-Ed Flipped Lessons: Yes, I Know My Students Are Prepared

Are your students prepared for class? With TED-Ed, you can create a set of online interactive questions that are embedded within the "flipped" video of your choice to ensure that your students do prerequisite work prior to entering your classroom. Instructors can then email the link to students or embed that link into a learning management system and collect the results. Anyone assigning a TED-Ed flip to students should be prepared for active learning in their face-to-face classroom. TED-Ed offers a free and simple-to-use process of "flipping" any YouTube video into a high quality lesson.

Overview

As instructors, we are asked to incorporate 21st-century skills into our courses; concurrently, a shift in the teacher-learner relationship has to take place. Does the modern student expect more variety and stimulation? With the ability to record and post lectures online, some instructors report that students are more prepared for class. Further, as collaborative classrooms, like those using PBL or TBL, gain favor, the unprepared student becomes a liability to his/her group. The TED-Ed lesson development tool, provided as a free service from TED.com, has features that enable the instructor to assign preparatory reading and video. The flipped lesson quiz is correlated using multiple choice, true-false, or short essay responses to assess each student's understanding of the material while providing a method of accountability.

Procedure

To help you learn how to use or create TED-Ed flips to engage your students, a step-by step guide is provided at the end of this tip, including links to the site's video tutorials. The starting point for using this tool is the TED-Ed website (http://ed.ted/org). With the free online tools there, instructors can flip any video that they create or they may utilize any existing content on YouTube! Through the TED-Ed flip tools, instructors can create questions in various formats (multiple choice, true/false, and essay) and attach those to a video. Instructors may also make use of discussion tools attached to the flipped video—and even offer extension tools where links to learn more may be shared. Even an option for collecting results exists.

Application

To enhance teaching method or strategy, instructors are able to post a TED-Ed flipped learning video assigned to their students prior to class sessions. The interactive questions connected to the video in the flip require and track student participation and offer formative feedback. Once the student receives the link to the lesson, he/she is able to watch the video, then move through the quiz. As soon as the student answers a question and submits the answer, instant feedback is provided. If the selected answer is incorrect, the student gets another opportunity to select the correct response. Corrective feedback is available by redirecting the student to specific times within the video that the instructor inputs so that remediation occurs. The completed quiz is submitted through the TED-Ed website. The results of each individual's quiz, as well as a composite of all students' scores, are provided to the instructor through TED-Ed.

Through the free TED-Ed resource, students watch a video lesson at home (anytime, anywhere), answer the questions, and then submit the completed video assessment. TED-Ed provides instructors with a URL (link) to share with students; that link can be pasted into an email, inserted as a link into a learning management system, or, if instructors require their students to create a free-login, TED-Ed is capable of scoring each individual quiz, then providing the results, both for the individual and for the entire group.

After assigning a flip, what happens back in the classroom? You can prepare to turn your face-to-face meetings into more hands-on, 21st-century active learning. Ed.TED. com is also a site that students can use to create and share their own flipped resources with peers as a means to enhance learning. Possibilities and variations abound. To begin creating your own TED-Ed flips, a brief guide follows.

References

Dweck, C. (2006). *Mindset: The new psychology of success*. New York: Random House.

Bellanca, J. A., & Brandt, R. S. (2010). *21st century skills: Rethinking how students learn*. Bloomington, IN: Solution Tree Press.

Bergmann, J., & Sams, A. (2012). *Flip your classroom: Reach every student in every class every day*. Eugene, OR: International Society for Technology in Education.

Pink, D. (2006). *A whole new mind: Why right-brainers will rule the future*. New York: Riverhead Books.

David Brobeck, Walsh University
Jacqueline Mumford, Walsh University

Using Animation to Display Course Content

As children, many students watched some form of animation on TV. Much of this animation consists of cartoons and other interactive programs where students can participate in the program in some way. However, animation can be used in the flipped college classroom to teach course content to students. I have used animation in my online classroom, and my students enjoy the fact that they can learn the concepts through the use of technology. Michael F. Ruffini (2009) reported his use of animation in slide presentations as a method to foster student engagement that enhances learning and retention of the instruction. Venable (2011) found that effective animations are designed to meet the needs of the learner audience, address specific learning objectives, and follow established design rules.

Recently, I have used a website called PowToon to create animations for my online mathematics courses. This website is interesting because of its option to choose a free-account or a paid account that has more features. I have used the free account, and I was able to move the character (instructor) around so that he could teach a certain section of the course. I was able to cover a topic in less than 25 slides. The best part is that the character is already created, and I can just type my information in the text boxes that are already provided. I can make the text boxes large or small. It is best to type no more than 3 sentences in each text box so that it is easy for students to read the material. I can transition the slides using animation techniques within the presentation. Also, I can decide how long each slide will stay on the screen. If more time is needed, I can adjust the time bar at the bottom of the screen. This website is an amazing resource because instructors can load their own audio into the presentation so that students can feel like they are being taught by their instructor. There is a library within the website where you use pictures and music or you can upload your own. After completing the presentation, an instructor can save it online for future access. If instructors want to send the presentation out to students, they can copy the link into their BlackBoard course or they can send it out to individual students. Overall, this website can be used by any instructor who is looking for a new way to present the course content to students. This form of technology can be viewed as a resource to students who are missing the face-to-face aspect of the mathematics classroom.

References

Ruffini, M. (2009, December). Creating animations in PowerPoint to support student learning and engagement. *EDUCAUSE Review,* 1-3. Retrieved from http://www.educause.edu/ero/article/creating-animations-power-point-support-student-learning-and-engagement

Venable, M. (2011, July 15). *Student engagement and online learning.* Retrieved from http://www.onlinecollege.org/2011/09/19/student-engagement-and-online-learning/

Antoinette M. Davis, Eastern Kentucky University

V. Assessment of Class Effectiveness

Many of us are being asked to assess just about everything we do. The classroom is no different. If flipping the classroom does not encourage deep learning among students, why do it? Through this section, we acknowledge the many possibilities for assessment in the flipped classroom, from specific activities to entire classes and the design of learning outcomes.

This section offers perspective on assessments for the flipped classroom. While assessments can include a variety of activities, the tips assembled here include suggestions for using reflection in the flipped classroom to examining the effectiveness of flipped strategies. The tips contained in this section encourage you to hone your skills as a flipped classroom instructor while offering opportunities to explore data-driven options for examining the success of your courses.

Blended Classes Relative to Traditional Classes: Perception and Performance Data

Our university is in the process of determining the feasibility of a 4-day class structure. One proposed technique for implementing a 4-day class structure, which is a variation of the flipped classroom, is to utilize the online course management system for assignment distribution and completion in lieu of one in-seat meeting per week. During the online course session, students are provided a variety of learning opportunities, such as watching taped lectures or videos, reading relevant case studies, or reading an excerpt related to weekly course content. In general, students are required to submit a written assignment or discussion board posts related to the content. These online activities usually replace in-seat class sessions on Fridays, which is the worst attendance day of the week.

Our department agreed to conduct a pilot study on the effectiveness of the blended course format for students and professors. In particular, the purpose of the study was to determine whether differences in perception and performance exist across the blended versus traditional course format. During the final week of the semester prior to final exams, students were asked to rate the blended course format relative to the traditional format in the department using a scale of worse, same, or better and then to explain the chosen rating. Department faculty also provided their perceptions regarding the pros or cons of the blended course format. After final exams were taken and graded, final exam grades were compared across sections of courses that were taught in both a traditional and blended manner.

When the performance data were analyzed, no significant differences in performance on final exams between classes taught in the traditional format as compared to classes using the flipped model were found. While this result may seem to be a non-significant (meaningful) outcome, from an academic and administrative perspective, it was actually quite interesting. The flipped model allowed instructors to actually cover more material by using the reading assignments and discussion board posts, and in their doing so students' test grades did not appear to suffer. Students were engaging the material independently and were able to translate that experience into acceptable academic performance. Textbook usage increased significantly because students were forced to use their texts to finish the assignments rather than depending on the professors to explain what the text material meant. In the yearly outcome assessment that the University conducts each year, student outcomes were comparable to those of previous years. We are expecting the outcomes for the national assessment used for our graduating seniors (ACAT exam) to improve over the next few years due to students being exposed to more of the concepts and content addressed on the test, as well as having numerous experiences where they are required to analyze and synthesize material from research and draw supportable conclusions. We will be monitoring that data for students who have used this model for all four years of their college as compared to those students who have only one year of this experience.

For preference data, over 80% of students (N = 138) rated the blended course as better, X^2 (2) = 138.65. One of the top reasons given for the better ratings was increased flexibility in scheduling, particularly for athletes and commuters, Given that a large percentage of students at our university are involved in intercollegiate athletics, and Friday is often a travel day for away games, not being required to be in-seat on Fridays allowed for more schedule flexibility. Similarly for commuters, one less trip to campus per week provided for increased schedule flexibility and reduced travel-related expenses and stressors. Also, students preferred the blended format because discussion board posts and related activities allowed students to better know what all class members thought. Many students reported that in many in-seat classes only a few students speak during class discussions because of class size or personality dispositions. Finally, students stated, without prompting, that they read the textbook more because the blended format placed more personal learning responsibility on them.

Although evidence existed that students liked the blended format, some students had indifferent or negative reactions. The top reasons given for the same and worse ratings were preference for lectures and technology problems. Those who reported a preference for lectures generally stated that lectures were of greater familiarity to them and they preferred professors to tell them what they need to know. The responses regarding technology problems generally involved problems with the course management system or on-campus computer networks.

Professors also rated the blended format as better. The primary reasons for the ratings included more time flexibility, increased personal responsibility in students, increased student interaction, increased student writing opportunities, covering more material in the course, and using the digital world to reinforce course concepts. Although faculty generally preferred the blended format, two primary cons were reported. The first con involved struggles about how to reframe or rethink the approach to teaching certain concepts in a blended format. For example, some research design and statistics concepts are less cumbersome to present in-seat relative to online. The second con involved an increased grading load. Even though not having a Friday in-seat meeting may appear to be an "off" day for faculty, the tradeoff is an increased volume of grading.

Eric Stephens, University of the Cumberlands
Dennis Trickett, University of the Cumberlands

Haley, Turner, University of the Cumberlands
Jane Moir Whitaker, University of the Cumberlands

Using Voicethread Case Study Design and Peer Analysis Within a Flipped Classroom Model

The purpose of this study was to examine the effects of employing various multimedia tools in a flipped classroom on pre-service teachers' self-efficacy and knowledge application abilities. The investigators employed a within-subject design with an independent variable: the flipped classroom or lecture-based instructional model and two dependent variables: (1) knowledge application of various multimedia tools and (2) students' perception of self-efficacy. The study participants included 36 senior-level elementary education majors from a medium-sized Mid-western university.

Findings

Collaborative Interaction and Application

Results from both the observational data and the survey findings showed students preferred hands-on, collaborative group work, stating that it, "enabled them to practice using the material they had learned in the chapter (and in class discussion). They also stated that it provided the opportunity to see the inherent challenges in certain practices, and they were able to discuss their ideas and impressions of these limitations with their classmates.

Metacognitive Self-Reflection

Another key theme that emerged was the importance of consistent, metacognitive self-reflection by the students regarding the learning process following each of the phases of the study. The role of metacognition in improving student outcomes emerged from the literature as one way to influence learning (Schraw, Crippen, & Hartley, 2006; Tanner, 2012), a theory that was supported in the study findings. More than 85% of the students commented that specifically focusing on the three areas: 1) what they learned, 2) how they learned it, and 3) what they needed to do in the future to improve their learning proved significantly more helpful than the traditional summative reflections they typically did in other courses, which usually only focused on the first area. For example, student 23 specifically stated that having this opportunity to reflect metacognitively at the conclusion of both of the phases (traditional versus flipped), really enabled her to think about how she learned best and to make measureable goals for how she could take more ownership of her learning in the future.

Instructors' "Theory of Action"

Argyris & Schön's (1997) 'theory of action' regarding espoused theory (what we say), versus our theories in use (what we do) was selected to illustrate the dichotomy in the findings regarding the instructor's use of power in the classroom and how it differed from phase 1 (traditional) to phase 2 (flipped). This concept of modeling how to use power 'with' versus 'over' others emerged multiple times in the data. Students reported in their reflections and in classroom discussions how much more they learned when the instructor acted as facilitator of learning in the class, asking questions to help motivate, guide, and empower them to work collaboratively with their peers versus simply standing at the front and lecturing from a PowerPoint, and being able to receive immediate feedback from their peers and their instructor really helped them to adjust their misconceptions and re-organize the new information for future use. (Bergmann & Sams, 2012; Bishop & Verlerger, 2013; Stayer, 2007). The data described the instructor's role in phase 2 (flipped) as hands-on; an active supporter of the learning process; consistently modeling those characteristics that the students felt were important for them to develop for use as future teachers with their own students.

Multimedia for Exploration and Expression

The final theme that emerged from the qualitative study findings and that concurred with the literature review was the important role multimedia played in improving students' self-efficacy (Baddeley, 1992; Mayer, 2003, 2005; Miler, 2005). Specifically, many of the students commented on how much they enjoyed working with their groups to explore the new multimedia tools like Voicethread and Gizmos and how much more interactive they were than just discussing a few pages from the course text. Nearly 100% of the students preferred the self-paced opportunity (Mayer, Dow & Mayer, 2003) that Quizlet provided to review the course material. Student 31, who had given herself a 6 on the Phase 1 self-efficacy pre-test and an 8 on the post-test, earning a 77% on the summative quiz, went up to a 7 on the pre-test during Phase 2 and a 9 on the post test and a 100% on the summative quiz. In her post comments she stated that being able to utilize the multimedia tools, especially Voicethread, "made the information come alive, I really felt like I could understand the problem more by being able to see and hear the teacher describing it. I loved using this program!"

The Voicethread case study activity consisted of the following elements. First the students interviewed their practicum teacher using the Voicethread application. Students asked their practicum teachers to read through the six course objectives (i.e., planning, reasoning, problem solving, positive attitude, adapting for diverse students, instructional techniques/technology, effective family Involvement, and reflective thinking) and select which one they thought posed the greatest challenge for new teachers. Then once the teacher had selected the problem area, the students, using the video option of Voicethread, recorded their teacher describing the problem and how it pertained to his/her unique classroom demographics. Once the students had recorded the interview, they posted the URL for their Voicethreads on the Blackboard discussion board. The second part of this assignment was that students were assigned to watch one of the practicum teacher interviews, and then, based on the problem described, they were to video record themselves describing various, specific solutions for the problem outlined. Their solutions could be based on information they had gleaned from the course, class materials, or other reliable sources. Rubrics for both parts of the assignment interview and peer case analysis were provided.

References

Argyris, D. & Schon, A. (1997). *Organizational learning: A theory of action perspective*. Reading, Mass: Addison and Wesley.

Baddeley, A. (1992). Working memory. *Science*, 255, 556-559.

Bergmann, J. & Sams, A. (2012). Flip Your Classroom: Reach Every Student in Every Class Every Day. Washington, DC: International Society for Technology in Education.

Bishop & Verlerger, 2013.

Mayer, R. (2003). *Learning and Instruction*. Upper Saddle River, NJ: Prentice Hall.

Mayer, R. (2005). Introduction to multimedia learning in R.E. Mayer (Ed.). *The Cambridge Handbook of Multimedia Learning*. New York: Cambridge University Press.

Mayer, R., Dow, G. & Mayer, S. (2003). Multimedia learning in an interactive self-explaining environment: What works in the design of agent-based micro-worlds? *Journal of Educational Psychology*, 95, 806-813.

Pajares, F. U. T. C. (2006). Self-efficacy beliefs of adolescents. From http://site.ebrary.com/id/10429529

Schraw, G., Crippen, K., & Hartley, K. (2006). Promoting self-regulation in science education: Metacognition a part of a broader perspective on learning. *Research in Science Education*, 36: 111-139.

Strayer, J. (2007). The effects of the classroom flip on the learning environment: a comparison of learning activity in a traditional classroom and a flip classroom that used an intelligent tutoring system.

Aileen J. Watts, Arkansas Tech University

Using Cognitive Coaching in a Flipped History and Contemporary Influences of Health, P.E. and Sport Classroom

Through an intense focus on developing critical thinking, student creativity, and problem solving using clarity, discernment, and integration, student learning will improve. The use of *Cognitive Coaching* (Costa, 2002), reflection assignments, class and small group discussion, articles, videos, TED talks, guest speakers, a PowerPoint assignment, and group assignments, all designed to enhance creativity and critical thinking, was employed in a "flipped classroom" design so that students would expand on their abilities to use creative and critical thinking to solve everyday problems.

The flipped course included students from various majors in the Health, Exercise, and Sports Science Department at the University of the Cumberlands. Students participated in the baseline and in the final data collection. In the beginning, there was little to no emphasis on clarity, discernment, and integration in the critical thinking process, but group work, discussion, videos, articles, reflections, quizzes, and PowerPoint assignments were measured by student progress in areas of content knowledge and critical thinking ability. These assignments occurred during each class. A baseline was developed to measure critical thinking once the students seemed to be comfortable with the class and the expectations of them throughout the course. For the baseline, students were asked to watch a video (Herr, 2014). Then they were asked to reflect in class on the video, using notebook paper and pencil/pen. No prompting regarding critical thinking was given. The responses were scored using a critical thinking rubric designed for the course. The students were then given various assignments throughout the semester that focused on developing critical thinking skills (reflection assignments, class and smaller group discussion, articles, videos, TED talks, a guest speaker, a PowerPoint assignment, and group assignments). The intensity of focus on clarity, discernment, and integration gradually increased due to intentional integration of these core concepts into the curricula. This integration was accomplished through reminders of what these critical thinking skills looked like and sounded like in writing, and through the use of Cognitive Coaching in the classroom. An example of one critical thinking assignment used throughout the semester is a reflection on news articles addressing ethics in sports. Another example of critical thinking assignments includes *Class Professional Goals* that were developed by the class through class discussion over current trends in Physical Education and sport. The assignment questions were based on a Cognitive Coaching reflecting conversation. For the Post-test, another TED talk was viewed (Epstein, 2014). Students were again asked to reflect in class on the video, using notebook paper and pencil/pen. Again, no prompting regarding critical thinking was given. The responses were scored using the same critical thinking rubric used for the pretest.

Data were scored and reported in a Microsoft Excel spreadsheet. Students' individual scores, averages, and class totals were included. The total individual and total class changes were also recorded. Overall, 19 students showed improvement in their average critical thinking ability while 4 students showed decline. The decline was due to a lack of understanding of the assignment during pre/post testing. The 23 class members as a whole improved 18.71 points for a 0.81 average improvement overall. The findings support that focused work in the area of critical thinking will help to improve overall student critical thinking. While students did not seem to find enjoyment in this type of "flipped classroom" work due to the additional work outside of the classroom and the lack of lectures over topics, the nonverbal cues given during Cognitive Coaching conversation and the results from the data collected support that learning occurred. Integrating Cognitive Coaching, critical thinking assignments, and discussions into the classroom was not difficult, although the time required for grading, assignments, and class discussions must be managed well. In the future, more focus will be put on critical thinking concepts earlier in the course, with clear intentions and expectations for higher quality work from students throughout the semester during critical thinking assignments. This approach should produce higher positive trends in the future.

Resources

Costa, Arthur L., and Robert J. Garmston. *Cognitive Coaching: A Foundation for Renaissance Schools*. 2nd ed. Norwood, MA: Christopher-Gordon P, 2002.

Epstein, David (2014).Are athletes really getting better, faster, stronger?: TED talk. http://www.ted.com/talks/david_epstein_are_athletes_really_getting_faster_better_stronger

Herr, Hugh (2014). The new bionics that let us run, climb, and dance: TED talk. http://www.ted.com/talks/hugh_herr_the_new_bionics_that_let_us_run_climb_and_dance

Sarah Adkins, University of the Cumberlands

Flipped Teaching Strategy with Preservice Teachers in a Technology Integration Course

To examine the effectiveness of the flipped teaching strategy with preservice teachers, I compared it with traditional teaching strategy on preservice teachers' learning outcomes, self-efficacy, and perception.

Participants

The participants were sixty preservice teachers (39 undergraduates, 21 graduates) enrolled in technology integration courses. The preservice teachers were non-science majors and attending three sections: Section one: 19 undergraduate students, Section 2: 20 undergraduate students and section three: 21 graduate students (10 male, 50 female). Students were from four different majors: 32 in early childhood education, 2 in elementary education, 14 in middle-level education, 9 in high school education, and 3 other education majors, such as physical education or speech/theater. English was reported as the native language of all participants. The average reported age of the participants was 22-25 years (SD = 1.415 years). Participants were 53 Caucasian, 4 African American, 1 Hispanic, and 1 Asian, among them 4 freshmen, 11 sophomores, 23 juniors, and 22 seniors.

The lessons and activities used with all participants were adapted from the textbook *Integrating Educational Technology into Teaching* by Roblyer and Doering, Sixth Edition (2012). Participants were taught by two different methods: the traditional lecture-based method was used to teach one topic, learning with technology in special education, while the flipped-based method was used to teach four topics: technology tools for 21st-century teaching, hypermedia tools for 21st-century teaching, distance teaching and learning and the role of the Internet, and developing and using web-based learning activities and teaching.

Materials

The learning materials used with students were five topics to help preservice teachers to integrate technology in teaching. The materials were identical in all sections and released every week with the related activities.

In the flipped teaching strategy, the following occurred: students read the chapter or online materials before class (at home). For the difficult points, students were asked to watch video or screencast. To ensure that students completed the assigned readings or videos, the instructor conducted a Q & A in the first five minutes of the class and then introduced the assigned topic in another five minutes. The instructor dedicated the class time to hands-on activities. Students worked through activities related to the assigned topic with the guidance of the instructor and the support of their peers. In this method, the instructor emphasized collaborative learning, and students had the opportunity to ask questions to the instructor and their peers as well. For example, in the flipped teaching strategy, the instructor started the topic "Distance teaching and learning and the role of the Internet" by asking students questions based on the home reading, such as why teachers should develop a rationale to use the Internet or what are some of the Internet's problem areas teachers have to address before using the Internet for teaching and learning? Students' answers included accessing sites with inappropriate materials, safety and privacy issues for students, fraud, computer viruses and hacking, and copyright and plagiarism issues. After the Q & A, the instructor introduced the topic using short PowerPoint presentations to cover the following points: "Distance education: an evolving use of the Internet, developing an Internet use rationale," and "using and implementing the Internet effectively: navigation, searching and storing, communicating and social networking." After the Q & A and the topic introduction, students were guided to complete hands-on activities related to the week's topic. For example, student were asked to develop a WebQuest, including: deciding the lesson to be taught through the WQ, using Google to collect the information web links, producing images and videos, and, finally, creating a free website for the WQ that includes: Introduction, Task, Process, Resource, Evaluation, Conclusion and Teacher Page. During the activity, students were free to ask for help or ask questions from their peers or instructor.

The traditional method was based on lectures and direct teachings conducted by the instructor, and the information was delivered during the meeting, while students listened to lectures and learned from them. In this method, the lesson's content and delivery were the most important aspects of instruction, and students learned knowledge through the assignments completed at home.

Flipped Method Works Better

The main finding of this experiment was that the use of the flipped teaching strategy has helped preservice teachers to improve their learning outcomes in the technology integration course. This enhanced benefit was demonstrated by the statistically significant differences in learning outcomes between students taught by flipped and lecture-based teaching strategies, with the highest scores achieved by students in the flipped condition.

Specifically, the preservice teachers' test scores improved on all tests after they engaged in flipped teaching activities compared to their test scores after lecture-based activities. A possible interpretation of this result is that students in the flipped classroom had the opportunity to work together and engage in hands-on learning activities, which allowed them to participate in an authentic and collaborative learning environment.

Furthermore, assigning multimedia learning materials for students to review outside the classroom allows them to learn content at their own pace and permits them to review those sections that present important or complex concepts (Gibbons Jf, 1977). This result is consistent with prior cognitive research, which noted the positive effect of allowing students to control the pace or stream of learning content. If students lack control over the pace of the learning content, their limited cognitive resources might be burdened, especially learning from multimedia materials. According to cognitive theory of multimedia learning (CTML), the human cognitive system can process only small portions of the large amounts of visual and auditory stimuli received. Unlike processing printed text, learners in a formal educational context typically do not have the opportunity to stop the multimedia presentation and reflect on what they are learning and identify potential gaps in their knowledge. Thus, information processing in this situation frequently requires longer and more intense periods of cognitive and metacognitive activity. Regardless of the amount of information presented in each sensory channel, the learner's working memory (WM) will accept, process, and send to long-term memory (LTM) only a limited number of information units (Attneave, 1954; Jacobson, 1950, 1951). Thus, working memory requires pauses or direct prompting to accept, process, and send to the long-term storage only the most crucial information (Clark, Nguyen, & Sweller, 2006).

Another significant finding of this experiment is that students' self-efficacy perception was significantly improved after engaging in flipped teaching strategy compared to their self-efficacy perception after lecture-based. This benefit was demonstrated by the statistically significant differences in the reported self-efficacy scores after the flipped activities compared to lecture-based, with the highest scores reported by students after the flipped activities.

Finally, this experiment found that preservice teachers favor the use of flipped teaching strategy in a technology integration course compared to the lecture-based teaching strategy. This preference was demonstrated by the statistically significant differences in the number of students who were in favor of the flipped strategy compared to lecture-based: (452 vs. 104) or (62.90% vs.14.50%).

A possible interpretation for this result could be drawn from students' justifications of their choices. Although the majority of students who preferred the flipped classroom indicated that it promotes collaboration and hands-on activities during the class time, other students have different reasons, such as: "had less lecture time," "work at my own pace," "using technology," "being able to interact more with the teacher and being able to ask questions as I worked" and "that we do not have to sit and listen to an hour long lecture that goes in one ear and out the other one."

Although opinions tended to be positive, invariably a few students strongly disliked the change. One very interesting case was a student who reported that she disliked the flipped teaching model because "Everyone is asking questions. I wasn't able to concentrate and do my work in the classroom. I am a very ADD person. I have to be somewhere without distractions to do well." Although this student reported her dislike of the flipped teaching model, she received higher grades on all the quizzes completed after flipped classes compared to her quiz grade after the lecture-based class.

References

Attneave, F. (1954). Some informational aspects of visual perception. *Psychological Review, 61*(3), 183-193.

Clark, Nguyen, & Sweller. (2006). *Efficiency in learning: Evidence-based guidelines to manage cognitive load*: Pfeiffer.

Gibbons Jf, K. W. R. D. K. S. (1977). Tutored videotape instruction: a New use of electronics media in education. *Science (New York, N.Y.), 195*(4283), 1139-1146.

Jacobson, H. (1950). The informational capacity of the human ear. *Science (New York, N.Y.), 112*(2901), 143-144.

Jacobson, H. (1951). The informational capacity of the human eye. *Science (New York, N.Y.), 113*(2933), 292-293.

Roblyer, M. D., & Doering, A. H. (2012). *Integrating Educational Technology into Teaching + Myeducationlab With Pearson Etext*: Allyn & Bacon.

Mohamed Ibrahim, Arkansas Tech University

VI. Assessment of Student Learning

On our campus, recent conversations have focused on assessing student learning. We even have a campus-wide Assurance of Learning Day each fall semester. Assessing learning is critical to any course or program. Building on the Assessment of Class Effectiveness section, the final section in the collection focuses on the assessment of student learning. This section offers tips on assessing mastery in student learning, using Bloom's Taxonomy as a guide for assessing student learning, and using tests in the flipped classroom. Other tips prompt us to pose questions, such as how do we assess mastery in student learning?

We hope that this section will encourage you to consider or reconsider your assessment as you design your flipped classroom. You might also ask: What experiences will you construct for your students? What are the affordances offered through the flipped classroom model? While assessing student learning can be a challenge, especially in what might be a new classroom design for you and your students, selecting modules or smaller sections of your class to assess might offer some comfort before attempting to assess every aspect. This section offer tips on how to begin to assess student learning in the flipped classroom.

Flipping Assessment in the Flipped Classroom: Using Bloom's Taxonomy as a Guide

Flipped classrooms naturally present unique opportunities for both formative or low-risk assessment (i.e., on-going evaluation of student progress in learning material) and summative assessment (i.e., evaluating comprehensive student learning of material at the end of a unit) to evaluate student learning both outside and inside the classroom. Conceptualizing assessment in a flipped classroom using Bloom's Taxonomy can be very useful to tailor evaluation to the aim of student learning throughout the course.

Outside of class, students are being asked to review foundational information. This information falls at the lower end of Bloom's Taxonomy, requiring students to learn basic definitions or processes. For example, reading materials, listening to lectures, or watching videos may be several ways in which students acquire such knowledge. To ensure that students learn this foundational information, assessment becomes a critical tool. Asking students to complete brief objective quizzes outside of class or at the beginning of the class session can increase the odds that students have completed this work without adding a significant grading burden to the instructor.

Inside of class, students focus on higher levels of Bloom's Taxonomy, applying foundational information, comparing and contrasting, or integrating foundational material. Numerous options exist for assessing students' efforts. A common option is for instructors to use 'product-based' in-class activities, providing an individual grading option. By developing 'products,' students are assessed on how well they are able to engage in higher levels of Bloom's Taxonomy that are being emphasized in the classroom. Since these higher levels of Bloom's Taxonomy are more challenging for students to learn, it may be appropriate to mix both formative (i.e., low-risk classroom assessments) with summative assessments. A relatively easy way to accomplish this task is to ask students to work individually on a task prior to working with a partner or group. The individual or pair work becomes a formative assessment that students can then check with their partner or with a larger group; the summative assessment can then be provided for the partner checked or group-checked product.

We now provide one example from a graduate level psychological assessment course of how you might utilize flipped assessments in a flipped classroom. Outside of the classroom, students are asked to complete a "learning check" or brief assignment option through an online learning platform prior to coming to class that week. Students are asked to either write or video record a response to assess their preliminary, foundational knowledge of a particular psychological instrument. Whether the response is written or recorded, students describe their understanding of the purpose, format, etc. of the psychological instrument in their own words. Such an assignment provides a brief formative assessment that helps the instructor evaluate to what degree students understand the basic concepts. These basic concepts can later be built upon through higher levels of Bloom's Taxonomy when students arrive to the classroom.

Once in the classroom, students are asked to work on interpreting fake psychological assessment data, using an assessment tool addressed in their readings. This "real world" application can only be successfully completed if the basic knowledge *about* the psychological instrument was gained outside of the classroom. First, students work in pairs to interpret the test data. From there, pairs come together to form small groups to further review the interpretations. Once group members check their understanding or comprehension with one another, they are then asked to apply, analyze, and synthesize the information with the "client's" background to determine how clinical decisions may be made in a real world application. Once the task is completed, the groups report on their findings to the class as a whole. Students submit their notes both from their pair and group work to serve as a more summative assessment of their learning.

The daily assessments – both formative and summative – that can occur in the flipped classroom provide powerful indicators of how well students are learning. To ensure that students value in-class work as much as foundational information, students need to see that the skills being taught in-class are a major part of the summative evaluation for the class. If professors provide exams that only reflect the foundational material and do not require students to demonstrate the in-class, higher order levels of Bloom's Taxonomy, students will quickly learn that the in-class time is not valued by professors. Further, students may not acquire the valuable skills of taking the information provided within the classroom to the real world for which they are being trained. Assessing their readiness to do so using a variety of methods across the components of the flipped classroom may provide instructors timely feedback as to their effectiveness calibrated with Bloom's Taxonomy.

Nathanael G. Mitchell, Spalding University
Norah Chapman, Spalding University
Robin K. Morgan, Indiana University Southeast
Acknowledgement: Thanks to Dave Morgan, Ph.D. for his contributions to editing.

Flip a Class? Flip a Test!

In a flipped approach student-created exam formats hold potential as a high-risk, high-reward activity during the classroom portion. The risk lies in the crafting of appropriate exam questions; however, the reward is earned when student comprehension is exceptional enough to create useable assessment pieces. Various types of exam questions can be created, including multiple choice, matching, and fill in the blank. Often multiple choice exam questions are used, for ease of execution and grading. Consider interlacing opportunities for student multiple choice question creation into your already planned course work. Could this be an opportunity for students to earn extra credit? Could the students submit multiple choice questions as part of a quiz? Identifying room in your curriculum for student creativity may lead to big payoff in the end.

Use of student-generated questions has been described in the literature, primarily with creation of multiple choice questions (Pittenger 2011, Rash 1997). Various venues have used multiple choice questions, from online to didactic courses. In 2011, Pittenger and Lounsbery describe the use of student-generated multiple choice questions to engage students in course material. The authors taught an online orientation course, encompassing three different sections of material. Students viewed the online material and then created multiple choice questions that tied in the section objectives. Questions were graded by the course team using a rubric, and top performing questions were then used in a section quiz. Final course grades incorporated both the question creation assessment and quiz performance. Those students creating questions appropriate for use in the section quiz were awarded extra credit points. The authors highlight how use of this technique increased student engagement and students reported a better understanding of the online material. Outside the multiple choice arena, use of student-created assessment is sparse. The first reported experience with student created exams comes from a mathematics course (Rash 1997). Students completing the course were responsible for creating their own unique math problem focused around a singular topic. Students then submitted a verbal problem and solution to the course instructor for feedback. Following the feedback, the students were given the opportunity to incorporate the feedback and resubmit the student-created problem and corresponding answers. Problems created throughout the semester were compiled and given to the students as a study guide for the final exam. As with the previous report, an increase in student comprehension was noted.

Irrespective of where you incorporate student-created exam questions, clear direction must be provided prior to initiation. How do the students decide what material is important? The authors above focused the students around course objectives or singular topics. Additionally, students must be given guidelines regarding creation of appropriate exam material. For multiple choice questions, what is an appropriate distractor? Are there college or university requirements that must be met? Use of online resources or exam creation guides may be helpful to students creating questions for the first time.

If your course allows for even further expansion of student-created assessment, consider student-created oral exams. Oral exams are a powerful way to gauge understanding and encourage critical thinking, as discourse can uncover and correct false assumptions or provide insight to a student's thought process (Huxham 2012, Burke-Smalley 2014). Oral exams are dynamic processes, where wrong answers may be corrected to facilitate improved transition to the next concept (Roecker 2007). Oral presentations refine the oral communication skills which are essential for graduates and provide more authentic workplace readiness as well as inherent resistance to plagiarism. For example, a student creating and demonstrating a mock interaction between an employer and employee is more realistic than a written description of how the student may approach a situation and demonstrates that the student is savvy enough to independently identify possible workplace interactions. Similarly, oral presentation of a student-created patient case in a healthcare course would require the student to thoroughly understand the disease state or problem. Oral presentation of patient information and planned solution, including need and rationale for any further diagnostic tests or recommended therapies, allows the student to practice communication skills before involving real patients. With this method, the instructor is also able to better assess the readiness of the student for the workplace or experiential learning setting and to facilitate further educational experiences as necessary. Though oral presentations and exams may invoke more student anxiety as compared to written assessments, students perform better and have reported preferring the oral assessments due to perceiving this as a more "professional" approach (Huxham 2012).

Use of student-created exams may not lessen the faculty workload. A change in the distribution of work to help students with appropriate question creation and providing feedback during the process may take up the time otherwise used to write exam questions. As with most things, this task will likely require less time as the process becomes more familiar. If you plan to incorporate student-created oral exams, it is important to carefully consider facial or verbal cues in order to decrease the potential for "giving away" the answer and to improve reliability. Creation and use of specific and detailed rubrics may decrease the potential for bias and improve consistency.

We have had success with the use of these techniques in our courses and hope the same for you. Happy flipping!

References

Pittenger, AL, Lounsbery. "Student-Generated Questions to Assess Learning in an Online Oriendation to Pharmacy Course." *American Journal of Pharmaceutical Education* 2011;75(5) Article 94.

Rash AM. "An Alternative Method of Assessment: Using Student-Created Problems." *Primus* 1997; 7(1):89-95.

Huxham M, Campbell F, Westwood J. "Oral versus Written Assessments: A Test of Student Performance and Attitudes." *Assessment & Evaluation in Higher Education* 2012; 37(1):125-136.

Burke-Smalley LA. "Using Oral Exams to Assess Communication Skills in Business Courses." *Business and Professional Communication Quarterly* 2014; 77(3):266-280.

Roecker L. "Using Oral Examination as a Technique to Assess Student Understanding and Teaching Effectiveness." *Journal of Chemical Education* 2007; 84(10):1663-1666.

Sarah A. Nisly, Butler University
Kristen R. Nichols, Butler University

Practicing What I Preach: Flipping for Mastery Learning in Assessment

I teach a classroom assessment course that all undergraduate teacher education majors are required to take. As a core requirement, the students in the class are diverse in majors (Elementary Education, Special Education, Music Education, Middle Grades, Secondary, etc) and in program experience (some in their sophomore year, others in the last semester before student teaching). As part of this class, I emphasize a mastery learning approach whereby students are assisted in mastering each learning target before advancing to a more advanced target (Bloom, 1971; 1976). In our first class, I introduce my students to the concept during the discussion of the syllabus. In subsequent classes, we have several classroom discussions about the concept after students read articles and book chapters on learning targets and mastery learning. However, I find that students are better able to formulate an opinion about whether or not this concept will work for them as future teachers by actually experiencing it themselves. Therefore, from reading quizzes to major group projects, I plan experiences for my students to engage in mastery learning firsthand. I have found that using a flipped classroom is the most effective way to implement mastery learning. More specifically, I utilize a flipped classroom format to implement a cyclic process of stepped assignments, formative assessment, and high-quality corrective instruction (Bloom, 1984; Guskey, 2010).

As an example of this cyclic process, the first major project students work on is a performance assessment designed to develop the skills necessary for translating state standard course of study goals and objectives into appropriate assessment activities for evaluating student learning. The instructions, templates, and rubrics for this multistepped assignment are posted to the online classroom management program (CMP). Students are expected to read the assignment documents outside of class and formulate questions to ask me at the next class. After briefly reviewing the assignment and answering students' questions, I prompt students to begin work on the first part of the assignment in self-assigned groups during class. During this time, students are able to ask questions of each other and me regarding resources and clarification of expectations for the assignment. Students complete the first part of the assignment during and/or after class and post their final work to the CMP by the next day. Before the next class, within the CMP, I use the rubric given to students as a formative assessment to inform students on their learning progress with the first part of the assignment. In addition, I provide specific electronic feedback for students in the form of comments on their project work, also posted to the CMP.

During the following class period, the results of the formative assessment direct what students focus on. Students with few or no revisions, start work on the next part of the assignment. Students with several revisions, use teacher feedback to make changes with the added benefit of being able to ask me specific follow up questions. Students with numerous revisions meet with me for small group high-quality corrective instruction (not re-teaching). For example, on part one of the assignment, students are required to identify appropriate curricular standards for the creation of a content based assessment and a performance based assessment. Students delineate the standards into learning targets classified into categories based on readings from class. Oftentimes, high-quality corrective instruction for this part of the assignment includes connecting the classifications of learning targets to the revised Bloom's Taxonomy (Anderson, et al., 2001), which students learned about in a previous course. All students submit revisions to the CMP for another round of formative assessment and feedback from me. Since each part of the assignment builds on previous parts, subsequent parts of the assignment cannot be attempted until the previous part has been successfully completed. This cycle continues until students have effectively concluded all parts of the assignment. Students have a finite amount of time to successfully complete each part to guarantee that the class moves forward at approximately the same time.

Naturally, this approach calls for a great deal of consistent work on the part of the professor. However, by breaking the assignment into parts, I found that this process actually took less time in the long run versus having students complete all parts of the assignment before receiving feedback. Even more important is the response from the students. Student course evaluations revealed an overwhelmingly positive response. Specifically, students stated the mastery learning method alleviated stress throughout the semester, facilitated question-asking and inquiry with both classmates and the professor, and enabled them to focus on learning the material rather than their grade as an outcome.

References

Anderson, L. W., Krathwohl, D. R., Airasian, P. W., Cruikshank, K. A., Mayer, R. E., Pintrich, P. R., Raths, J., & Wittrock, M. C. (2001). *A taxonomy for learning, teaching, and assessing: A revision of Bloom's taxonomy of educational objectives, abridged edition.* White Plains, NY: Longman.

Bloom, B. S. (1971). Mastery learning. In J. H. Block (Ed.), *Mastery learning: Theory and practice* (pp. 47–63). New York: Holt, Rinehart and Winston.

Bloom, B. S. (1976). *Human characteristics and school learning.* New York: McGraw-Hill.

Bloom, B. S. (1984). The search for methods of group instruction as effective as one-to-one tutoring. *Educational Leadership, 41*(8), 4–17.

Guskey, T. R. (2010). Lessons of mastery learning. *Educational Leadership, 68*(2), 52–57.

Chrystal Dean, Appalachian State University

VII. For Further Reading and Research

As the Graduate Assistant for the Teaching & Learning Center and the Noel Studio for Academic Creativity, I assisted authors Charlie Sweet, Hal Blythe, and Russell Carpenter in creating this title by providing updated research on the topic of flipped learning. While researching flipped learning, I quickly realized that no universal way to implement flipped learning in the classroom exists, as many techniques for successful implementation have been proposed. Regardless of the approach used to implement flipped learning, research supports the following key concepts as integral to successfully applying the paradigm in the classroom:

1. Flipped learning is not about replacing teachers with technology, but it is about altering teachers' roles in the classroom. Through flipped learning, teachers facilitate student engagement and interaction, rather than lecture on vast amounts of content.
2. Flipped learning is not a suitable approach for every course, and teachers should carefully consider how the approach would or would not assist them in attaining the goals of the course.
3. Properly applying flipped learning in the classroom can require a significant amount of time and planning. Beginners should carefully consider the time commitment before implementing the approach.
4. Research supports that students' perceptions of flipped learning are generally positive. However, it is vital that teachers take time to gain students' support and buy-in for the flipped learning approach. Specifically, teachers should explain to students how the flipped learning approach will be applied in the classroom, what behaviors are expected of students, and how the approach will benefit students.

The following is a list of resources I gathered for the authors while researching flipped learning. I have provided annotations for the resources I found to be most educational and interesting. I hope these resources will assist you in determining if flipped learning is right for you.

Abeysekera, L., & Dawson, P. (2015). Motivation and cognitive load in the flipped classroom: definition, rationale and a call for research. *Higher Education Research & Development, 34*(1), 1-14. doi:10.1080/07294360.2014.934336

Andrejasich Gibes, E. E., & James, H. H. (2015). Is flipping enough? *College & Research Libraries News, 76*(1), 10-13.

Arnold-Garza, S. (2014). The flipped classroom teaching model and its use for information literacy instruction. *Communications In Information Literacy, 8*(1), 7-22.

Berrett, D. (2012). How 'flipping' the classroom can improve the traditional lecture. *Chronicle Of Higher Education, 58*(25), A16-A18.

Bishop, J. & Verlager, M.A. (2013). The flipped classroom: A survey of the research. *120th Annual ASEE Annual Conference & Exposition Available*, Atlanta, USA, 23-26th June.

Buemi, S. (2014). Microflipping: A modest twist on the 'flipped' classroom. *Chronicle Of Higher Education, 60*(32), 6.

- Sam Buemi proposes microflipping as an alternative approach to flipped learning. According to Buemi, increasing the amount of technology used in the classroom will not solve the age-old educational problem that some students come to class unmotivated or ill-prepared. Microflipping blends traditional-lecture approaches with flipped classroom techniques to enable teachers to instruct both prepared and unprepared students. Microflipping involves combining technology with student engagement while lecturing students on content in a conversation-style format. The benefit of microflipping, as opposed to flipped-learning, is that teachers can increase student engagement and critical thinking without completely altering their course structure. Microflipping enables teachers to add new pedagogical techniques to their classrooms in increments.

Carpenter, R. G., Blythe, H., Sweet, C., Winter, R., & Bunnell, A.(2015). A challenge for the flipped classroom: Addressing spatial divides. In A. G. Scheg (Ed.)*, Implementation and critical assessment of the flipped classroom experience* (pp.141-157).

Davies, R., Dean, D., & Ball, N. (2013). Flipping the classroom and instructional technology integration in a college-level information systems spreadsheet course. *Educational Technology Research & Development, 61*(4), 563-580.

EDUCAUSE Learning Initiative. (2012). 7 things you should know about flipped classrooms. *Educause.* Retrieved from http://net.educause.edu/ir/library/pdf/ELI7081.pdf

Enfield, J. (2013). Looking at the impact of the flipped classroom model of instruction on undergraduate multimedia students at CSUN. *Techtrends: Linking Research & Practice To Improve Learning*, *57*(6), 14-27. doi:10.1007/s11528-013-0698-1

Fautch J. M., (2014), The flipped classroom for teaching organic chemistry in small classes: is it effective? *Chem. Educ. Res. Pract.*, 16, 179–186.

Fickes, M. (2014). Flipping technology. *School Planning & Management*, *53*(11), 44.

Flipped Learning Done Right. (2014). *American School Board Journal*, *201*(6), 42.

- The editorial staff discusses the purpose of flipped learning and strategies for successful implementation. According to Doug O'Brien, Director of Strategic Business at TechSmith, flipped learning aims to increase student productivity so teachers can meet more students' learning needs. Due to teachers' overwhelming day-to-day task requirements, they are unable to attend to every student's needs. Flipped learning aims to solve this problem by enabling teachers to create lessons in advance and to use classroom time for exploring content more deeply. Flipped learning utilizes technology in a way that enables teachers to give students more individualized instruction. As the article states, teachers are the most important part of education and a university's biggest investment. By implementing flipped learning strategies, universities are investing in teachers' productivity and professional development.

Forsey, M., Low, M., & Glance, D. (2013). Flipping the sociology classroom: Towards a practice of online pedagogy. *Journal Of Sociology*, *49*(4), 471-485. doi:10.1177/1440783313504059

Francl, T. (2014). Is flipped learning appropriate? *Journal Of Research In Innovative Teaching*, *7*(1), 119-128.

Gilboy, M., Heinerichs, S., & Pazzaglia, G. (2015). Enhancing student engagement using the flipped classroom. *Journal of Nutrition Education and Behavior, 47*(1), 109-114. doi:0.1016/j.jneb.2014.08.008

- Gilboy, Heinerichs, and Pazzaglia document their template for designing a flipped learning classroom and its effects on students' perceptions. The authors' template for flipped learning involves three stages: before, during, and after class. Before class, students were instructed to acquire content knowledge through the use of online modules that included mini-lectures, technology or entertainment videos, worksheets, and written prompts. During class, students were divided into expert workgroups and instructed to work through critical thinking questions provided by the instructor and to make posters outlining their arguments. After the students completed the critical thinking questions, each workgroup presented their poster to the class. The last portion of the authors' flipped learning template involves an after-class assessment, which can be distributed to students in one of many forms: essay exam, case study, presentation, reflection paper, test creation, and group testing. Survey results revealed that students perceived this template for flipped learning favorably, for it allowed them to work at their own pace and gave them time to apply the content they learned. Criticisms of the template included concerns about not having the professor available to ask questions during the out-of-class portion and concerns over lack of other students' preparation. The implications from this approach to flipped learning are that digitalizing lectures and determining appropriate active learning strategies require extensive time and commitment from teachers, gathering student buy-in about the flipped learning process is vital to successful implementation, teachers should track student log-in and time spent in online modules to determine utilization and value of the videos, and modules should be limited to 10-15 minutes to minimize boredom and distractions and to maximize student engagement.

Goodwin, B. (2013). Evidence on flipped classrooms is still coming in. *Educational Leadership*, *70*(6), 78.

Gorman, M. (2012, July 18). 21st century educational technology and learning: Flipping the classroom…a goldmine of research and resources to keep you on your feet. [Web log comment]. Retrieved from: http://21centuryedtech.wordpress. com/2012/07/18/flipping-the-classroom-a-goldmine-of-research-and-resources-to-keep-you-on-your-feet/

Herreid, C., & Schiller, N. (2013). Case studies and the flipped classroom. *Journal of College Science Teaching*, *42*(5), 62-66.

Holmes, M. R., Tracy, E. M., Painter, L. L., Oestreich, T., & Park, H. (2015).Moving from flipcharts to the flipped classroom: Using technology driven teaching methods to promote active learning in foundation and advanced masters social work courses. *Clinical Social Work Journal,* 1-10.

Hung, H. (2015). Flipping the classroom for English language learners to foster active learning. *Computer Assisted Language Learning*, *28*(1), 81-96. doi:10.1080/095 88221.2014.967701

Jensen, J. L., Kummer, T. A., & Godoy, P. D. D. M. (2015). Improvements from a Flipped Classroom May Simply Be the Fruits of Active Learning. *CBE-Life Sciences Education*, *14*(1), ar5.

Kay, Y., & O'Malley, P. (2014). Making 'the flip' work: Barriers to and implementation strategies for introducing flipped teaching methods into traditional higher education courses. *New Directions (Higher Education Academy)*, *10*(1), 59-63. doi:10.11120/ndir.2014.00024

Mason, G. S., Shuman, T., & Cook, K. E. (2013). Comparing the effectiveness of an inverted classroom to a traditional classroom in an upper-division engineering course. *IEEE Transactions On Education*, *56*(4), 430-435. doi:10.1109/TE.2013.2249066

McLaughlin, J., Roth, M., Glatt, D., Gharkholonarehe, N., Davidson, C., Griffin, L., & ... Mumper, R. (2014). The flipped classroom: A course redesign to foster learning and engagement in a health professions school. *Academic Medicine: Journal Of The Association Of American Medical Colleges*, *89*(2), 236-243. doi:10.1097/ACM.0000000000000086

Moffett, J., & Mill, A. C. (2014). Evaluation of the flipped classroom approach in a veterinary professional skills course. *Advances In Medical Education & Practice*,*54*15-425. doi:10.2147/AMEP.S70160

Murray, D., Koziniec, T., & McGill, T. (2015). Student Perceptions of Flipped Learning.

- After applying flipped learning to an IT course, authors Murray, Koziniec, and McGill utilized an online survey to study students' perceptions of flipped learning. The results of the survey revealed that on average students found the flexibility of flipped learning to be favorable and had generally positive perceptions of flipped learning. In addition, students reported higher levels of interaction with instructors and peers despite face-to-face teaching time being reduced. Students most preferred computer-led videos where applied course elements were being demonstrated and discussed. Lastly, the results of the survey revealed that it is important for teachers to recognize their role as tutorial facilitators; flipped learning videos are not meant to replace instructors in the classroom.

Nielsen, L. (2012). Five reasons I'm not flipping over the flipped classroom. *Tech & Learning*, *32*(10), 46.

O'Flaherty, J. & Phillips, C. (2015). The use of flipped classrooms in higher education: A scoping review. *The Internet and Higher Education, 25*, 85-95.

Raths, D. (2014). Nine video tips for a better flipped classroom. *Education Digest*, *79*(6), 15.

Sams, A., & Bergman, J. (2013). Flip your students' learning. *Educational Leadership*, *70*(6), 16.

- The authors discuss the true purpose of flipped learning. Contrary to popular belief, flipping the classroom is not about incorporating more technology, but it is about making the most of in-class time and engaging students in higher-order thinking. Flipped learning creates a student-centered environment by giving teachers the flexibility to attend to each student's learning needs and by providing students with multiple ways to have their learning needs met. Sams and

Bergmann point out that flipped learning is not appropriate for every classroom. Flipped learning is most applicable to courses that supply large quantities of content and involve skills on the low end of Bloom's taxonomy, specifically remembering and understanding. Flipped learning enables teachers to incorporate higher-order thinking skills into these courses and portray the vast quantity of information in an engaging way.

Seyedmonir, B., Barry, K., & Seyedmonir, M. (2014). Developing a community of practice (CoP) through interdisciplinary research on flipped classrooms. *Internet Learning Journal*, *3*(1), 85-94.

Sonic Foundry, I. (2). D.I.Y. Video Lectures: Ball State University Uses My Mediasite as One-Stop-Shop for Flipped Learning. *Business Wire (English)*.

Talbert, R. (2012). Inverted classroom. *Colleagues 9*(1), Article 7: 1-4.

Talley, C., & Scherer, S. (2013). The enhanced flipped classroom: Increasing academic performance with student-recorded lectures and practice testing in a "flipped" STEM course. *Journal of Negro Education*, *82*(3), 339-347.

Young, J. R.(2015, January 16). A flipped-classroom 'rock star' hand off his video lectures. Then what? *The Chronicle of Higher Education*, pp. A13.

Kelsey Strong, Eastern Kentucky University

Take-Aways: Some Fundamental and Powerful Principles about Flipping the Classroom

Before we go, we'd like to offer you a summary of the best ideas about flipping the classroom (maybe someday some of these ideas will grow up to be best practices).

1. Most faculty have heard of the flipping approach; in fact, one study puts that number at 96%.

2. If you use the flipped approach, make your students aware from the beginning of your methodology—i.e., metacognition. Explain to them the pros and cons.

3. Experimenting with the flipped approach is O.K. Not all of your classes need to be flipped nor even all meetings of one class (as long as your students are clear on your approach). You might start by flipping certain modules.

4. Since your students don't have access to you while taking in the pre-class material, anticipate by being willing to ask and answer questions at the beginning of class. This suggestion is especially vital when you introduce something very new or very complex.

5. Use the 15-minute rule of structure. During class time, no single activity, including lecture, should take over 15 minutes. Emphasize variety.

6. With your in-class activities, try to emphasize Bloom's higher learning skills of applying, analyzing, evaluating, and creating over the lower order skills remembering and understanding.

7. No video can replace the instructor. Videos can't answer spontaneous questions or read the body language of the puzzled students.

8. Be flexible. Be willing to change your course based on your read of student learning or lack of it.

9. Don't feel you have to re-invent the wheel by constructing all your pre-class PowerPoints, videos, and other presentations on your own. However, you must make sure you have the legal right to use those things you borrow (e.g., the Khan Academy library of 3000 videos).

10. The jury on flipping the classroom is still out. Student satisfaction responses

seem to favor this approach, but studies of improved/deep learning are sketchy at best (see Bishop & Verleger 2013).

11. Flippers need support, and you may overwhelm the AV-competent crowd with your requests for help. Consider using students in your class or in an AV major to help you prepare the pre-class material.

12. If nothing else, flipping the classroom is a valuable approach because it moves users past the reliance on the traditional period-long lecture approach.

13. Monitor your students carefully. The flipping method puts more responsibility on their shoulders for learning.

14. Offer students opportunities to provide open and honest feedback about the flipped class approach.

15. Treat your students as allies—i.e., co-facilitators of knowledge—in your flipped courses. They can help your improve your instruction.

16. Test your flipped course—or specific assignments—in advance with colleagues or students you trust.

17. Develop familiarity with the technology you plan to use in your flipped course in advance. Try new technologies during the summer or when you have time to experiment.

18. Keep up with the latest trends in open-source or freely available technology. Consider linking online modules or lessons with technology that students know, even social media.

19. Evaluate the affordances of multimedia, and weigh the opportunities of using mediated communication such as video compared to audio or text files.

20. Instructors of flipped classrooms should manage online content closely. It is easy for online and face-to-face content to feel disconnected or unrelated for students. Ensure that each online module connects back to the most recent face-to-face class, even if content was created in advance of the semester.

About the Authors

Hal Blythe, Ph.D. (University of Louisville, 1972), is the Co-Director of the Teaching & Learning Center at Eastern Kentucky University. With Charlie, he has collaborated on over 1200 published works, including 17 books (eight in New Forums' popular It Works For Me Series), literary criticism, and educational research.

Charlie Sweet, Ph.D. (Florida State University, 1970), is the Co-Director of the Teaching & Learning Center at Eastern Kentucky University. With Hal, he has collaborated on over 1200 published works, including 17 books, literary criticism, educational research, and ghostwriter of the lead novella for the *Mike Shayne Mystery Magazine*.

Russell Carpenter, Ph.D. (University of Central Florida, 2009), directs the Noel Studio for Academic Creativity and Minor in Applied Creative Thinking at Eastern Kentucky University where he is also Assistant Professor of English. He is the author or editor of several recent books including *The Routledge Reader on Writing Centers and New Media* (with Sohui Lee), *Cases on Higher Education Spaces*, *Teaching Applied Creative Thinking* (with Charlie Sweet, Hal Blythe, and Shawn Apostel), and the *Introduction to Applied Creative Thinking* (with Charlie Sweet and Hal Blythe). He serves as President of the Southeastern Writing Center Association and Past Chair of the National Association of Communication Centers.

Made in the USA
Middletown, DE
24 January 2016